FICTION RUINED
MY FAMILY

FICTION RUINED MY FAMILY

Jeanne Darst

RIVERHEAD BOOKS   _a member of Penguin Group (USA) Inc. New York 2011_

RIVERHEAD BOOKS

Published by the Penguin Group
Penguin Group (USA) Inc., 375 Hudson Street, New York, New York 10014, USA
Penguin Group (Canada), 90 Eglinton Avenue East, Suite 700, Toronto, Ontario
M4P 2Y3, Canada (a division of Pearson Penguin Canada Inc.) • Penguin Books
Ltd, 80 Strand, London WC2R 0RL, England • Penguin Ireland, 25 St Stephen's
Green, Dublin 2, Ireland (a division of Penguin Books Ltd) • Penguin Group
(Australia), 250 Camberwell Road, Camberwell, Victoria 3124, Australia (a divi-
sion of Pearson Australia Group Pty Ltd) • Penguin Books India Pvt Ltd, 11
Community Centre, Panchsheel Park, New Delhi–110 017, India • Penguin
Group (NZ), 67 Apollo Drive, Rosedale, North Shore 0632, New Zealand (a divi-
sion of Pearson New Zealand Ltd) • Penguin Books (South Africa) (Pty) Ltd, 24
Sturdee Avenue, Rosebank, Johannesburg 2196, South Africa

Penguin Books Ltd, Registered Offices: 80 Strand, London WC2R 0RL, England

Library of Congress Cataloging-in-Publication Data

Darst, Jeanne.
    Fiction ruined my family / Jeanne Darst.
        p.   cm.
    ISBN 978-1-59448-814-6
    1. Darst, Jeanne—Childhood and youth.   2. Darst, Jeanne—Homes and haunts.
3. Novelists, American—21st century—Biography.   I. Title.
PS3604.A78Z46   2011   2011027830
813'.6—dc22

Printed in the United States of America
10 9 8 7 6 5 4 3 2 1

BOOK DESIGN BY NICOLE LAROCHE

While the author has made every effort to provide accurate telephone numbers
and Internet addresses at the time of publication, neither the publisher nor the
author assumes any responsibility for errors, or for changes that occur after publication. Further, the publisher does not have any control over and does not assume
any responsibility for author or third-party websites or their content.

Penguin is committed to publishing works of quality and integrity.
In that spirit, we are proud to offer this book to our readers;
however, the story, the experiences, and the words
are the author's alone.

For Liz

And, no bout a doubt it, for Dad

CONTENTS

AUTHOR'S NOTE

Tennessee Williams said, "Memory is seated predominantly in the heart." What he meant by this was, fuck off. I like to think I'm considerably less testy than "the Glorious Bird," so what I'd like to say regarding accounts and versions of the truth that may differ slightly from mine in this book is: I don't have the greatest memory. So, this stuff is true, but I don't claim any talent as a stenographer. I have also changed the names and identifying characteristics of some people to protect their privacy.

FICTION RUINED
MY FAMILY

FICTION RUINED
MY FAMILY

WRITERS TALK A LOT about how tough they have it—what with the excessive drinking and three-hour workday and philandering and constant borrowing of money from people they're so much better than. But what about the people married to writers? Their kids? Their friends? Their labradoodles? What happens to them? I'll tell you what happens to them. They go fucking nuts. Tolstoy's wife, Sophia, after copying *War and Peace*—1,225 pages—by hand seven times and having thirteen children by him, is rumored to have poisoned him in his eighty-second year; Viv Eliot, institutionalized after being found meandering the streets of London at five a.m. asking if T.S. had been beheaded, died in Northumberland House mental hospital, after one failed escape attempt, at age fifty-eight; William Makepeace Thackeray's wife, Isabella, threw herself out of a bathroom window on a ship at sea headed for Ireland rather than vacation with him.

One might almost judge writers not by their prose but by the people around them. How nuts are they?

My father is a writer, and so were both his parents. As a

kid, I suspected writing might be what was causing my family to implode.

But beyond the actual writing there was a broader kind of storytelling that seemed to define us. The family myth—stories of who we were—informed everything. My father came from an old Missouri family that arrived in Maryland on the *Dove* in 1634. My great-great-great-grandfather John Paul Darst was the carpenter and contractor on the Old Cathedral in St. Louis in 1830. We were prominent Democrats. My great-uncle Joe Darst was mayor of St. Louis in the late 1940s. My grandmother Katharine Darst had a daily column in the *St. Louis Globe-Democrat* called "Here and There" and a Sunday column called "The Back Seat Driver." My grandfather James Darst, a dashing newspaperman whom family members called Dagwood or Dag, wrote pretty awful plays and very good short stories when he wasn't working for Fox Movietone News. And my father, a reporter, had been an alderman in St. Louis in the '60s with an eye toward being mayor before he quit politics to write.

My mother's family, on the other hand, was rich in a thing called money from her father's ophthalmology practice in St. Louis. Her childhood was one of mass before Catholic school and winning horse shows around the country on weekends, until she and her sister Ruth landed on the cover of *Sports Illustrated* at ages fourteen and seventeen, respectively, and then zoomed off in T-Birds bought by "Daddy" to debutante balls, a women's college in the East, and marriage. Wild-rich-girl stuff.

What these stories seemed to be saying to me, growing up, was: things aren't going that great now, but it's all about to change, drastically, because Dad's gonna sell this novel, this is the one, and there'll be no more scraping by, no more walking home from school in January in a thin jacket and no gloves pretending you're not cold. Mom will be restored to her former fanciness and will become undepressed and able to drink normally, as happens with literary success, and Dad will have fulfilled his lifelong dream and in doing so will stop driving everyone bananas. It seemed my parents were willing to suffer, make others suffer, and even die to maintain these impossible fantasies—even after my father eventually stopped doing any actual writing at all (not that anyone ever acknowledged this) and the fantasies were all that was left. My parents slowly lost everything and fell apart. As an adult, it's hard not to wonder how people with their kind of talent, charm, intelligence and privileged backgrounds could wind up like them.

And then I became a writer, too. An alcoholic, broke, occasionally irresistible, destructive, quasi-adult—one who believed that writing was at least partly what was causing my life to fall apart but also that it was what would redeem it in the end. Another generation of the stories, fantasies and delusions. Ultimately, I sobered up and began actually writing instead of just talking about it, ever so narrowly avoiding repeating the exact—and I mean exact—mistakes of my mother and father. I became very much like them without becoming exactly like them. This was possible, I believe, through no moral superiority of mine and certainly no more talent than my father, but through the odd fortune of being able to see the truth and, having done that, use it to move forward. I have managed to become an artist and not lose my mind or cause others to lose theirs. I work in stories but I live in reality. Or at least, that's the tale I now tell myself.

ONE YEAR IN
NEW YORK

J UNE 1976. We were moving from St. Louis to Amagansett for a year so my dad could write his novel, *Caesar's
Things*, about a senator who has a nervous breakdown after
being involved in a love triangle with a debutante and his
own father, which comes to light years later when he is cam-
paigning for president.

My mother's mother didn't want us to go and tried to haggle
with my dad for my oldest sister, Eleanor, as we were leaving.
The four of us girls were staking out our turf in the car, laying
out candy we had just bought at the Rexall on Clayton Road
to determine the order of consumption for the thousand-mile
drive, when Nonnie walked over to the car, adjusted her big
tortoiseshell frames as if getting ready to start a press confer-
ence, and said to my father, "Eleanor does not want to go to
New York. Eleanor should stay with me. She'll have a better
life here with me, food at regular hours, not at midnight and
whatnot, and she'll go to mass regularly and attend the

Annunziata school, and she'll be bathed properly, and she likes to watch Johnny Carson with us here on Friday nights." I thought my dad should take her up on it, I mean, why not? Eleanor loved watching Johnny Carson with Nonnie and her sister Neallie on Nonnie's big bed and having Jell-O boats at Stix, Baer & Fuller after some shopping. This was maybe not the profile of someone who wanted to head off into a year of "getting the novel together" on some remote farm halfway across the country. Now, I was up for New York, I was up for the ocean and living on a farm, which I would quickly discover had more *New Yorker* writers on it than cows or chickens, but I was ready to go and if Eleanor couldn't cut it, well, we'd see her in a year, now let's get going. St. Louis sucks, especially in the airless, way back of our station wagon.

My dad said he was taking all his kids with him, thank you, Mrs. Gissy, and "Let's not get so damn dramatic, everybody," we would all be back next spring. "It's one year in New York." My mother was crying, not because she didn't want to go to New York; she did. She just had a light cry going most of the time, one that didn't require a hanky, just a smooth stroke across her cheek to keep moving through the day. Like Seattlers who as a point of pride don't use umbrellas in their eternally drippy town, my mother hissed if you offered up a Kleenex, the tool of tourists.

My grandmother walked around to the back of the car, leaned in the back window and said in full voice, "Anyone who wants to come back to St. Louis can come back and have their own room in my house, no questions asked. You've all memorized my phone number, so just call collect. Don't worry, girls."

It was easy to tell that my grandmother didn't see this as a worthy adventure. I don't remember any books in her house at all, other than the children's books in the playroom she kept for her twelve grandchildren and the medical books my deceased grandfather left behind in the office where she paid bills and cut checks to charities like the St. Louis Society for the Blind. I never saw her read anything except *Reader's Digest*. Seeing a copy of *The Grapes of Wrath* in her living room would have been like spotting a dead falcon on her coffee table. Maybe if my father were writing a novel in Braille, Nonnie would have seen some value in it, but as it was, he was ruining my mother's life, taking her away from everything that meant anything—her. Nonnie looked at my father. She blew a kiss into the backseat.

"I'll see you girls very soon."

"Bye, Nonnie," we said brightly, and waved, her words leading us to believe we were heading off on some kind of scavenger hunt, a yearlong one that would wind up with us watching a rousing game of bridge in her living room with her best pal, Monsignor Hartnett, and her do-gooding friends from Annunziata Church, smoking Carltons and having a Tom Collins or two.

"Good-bye, Mother," my mother sighed. Although she was psychologically duct-taped to her mother, I never saw them physically touch. (I, on the other hand, was fine with symbolic behavior. By this age, seven, I had only recently stopped sucking on my mother's neck at night while we all watched television.)

"Verena," my father said, a verbal tip of the hat, and hit the gas as if we had the kind of car that could perform in a peel-out.

Our green, wood-paneled Ford Torino wagon reached the East End of Long Island in early summer. The local white corn, tomatoes, and gin and tonics would soon be coming up. A friend of my father's from St. Louis, a preposterously tan writer named Berton Roueché, had arranged a house for us. It was a small, two-story converted horse barn on Stony Hill Farm in Amagansett. The farm was surrounded by potato fields. There was a handwritten wooden sign nailed to a tree at the entrance that read STONY HILL FARM. A woman named Penny Potter owned the place. (My dad would later tell Penny Potter to go fuck herself, when she didn't invite my parents to cocktails until three months after we had arrived from St. Louis. In my father's opinion, "Go fuck yourself" was the only civilized response to bad manners.)

Penny had been married to a writer named Jeffrey Potter. Writer Peter Matthiessen and his wife had lived in what was now our house. The hill house was the storied spot where Arthur Miller and Marilyn Monroe spent the summer of 1957, arriving by helicopter on the front field. When people came from St. Louis to visit, my dad gave them the dead-artists-and-writers tour, driving them to the Green River Cemetery, where A. J. Liebling and Jackson Pollock and Stuart Davis were buried, highlighting the curve on Fireplace Road where Pollock cracked up.

My mother wasn't thrilled about leaving her mother for a year, but she was up for a place with more scope and more glamour. Both my parents wanted a bigger game, and New York was it. And Dad was about to be it. He had been selling pieces to *Harper's*, *The Atlantic Monthly*, and the *New York Times Magazine*, and the great literary novel was the next obvious step. She believed in him.

Besides the Rouechés, the other friends my parents spent time with were more writers, like Mike Mooney, Willie Morris, Martin Quigley and Eloise Spaeth, an industrialist's widow and art collector whom my parents also knew from St. Louis. Mrs. Spaeth and her late husband had been huge figures in the New York art world in the '50s and '60s, involved in promoting artists like Picasso, Calder, and Willem de Kooning. Mrs. Spaeth was a big deal at the Whitney, and she lived in a modern house that had art and sculpture everywhere, like the Picasso birdbath out by the pool. She was respected for her impeccable taste and vision, and I thought it must mean Dad was really up-and-coming if she was friends with him.

Everyone was "interesting": "Hell of an interesting gal, very bright, has a piece in *The New Yorker*, is researching something terrific, was friendly with so-and-so, working on a collection of stories." It seemed there was no shortage of little stories about the writers and artists who lived around us. "Quigs [my father's friend Martin Quigley] said he used to ride the train with Pollock. 'Jack and I used to drink together in the bar car of the Montauk Cannonball.'" They called it that because it was the slowest train of all time. Big, black, slow.

"Saul Steinberg, who lives down the road from Quigs, calls Martin's wood-burning stove 'the black cat,'" my father would tell his old friend Hereford on the phone.

My parents had a cocktail party one night, and my dad pulled me aside and said, "Now, Jean, there's a woman coming over tonight and I want you to pay attention to her, to what she's like, because you'll read *Tender Is the Night* someday and the couple in it, the Divers, were based on her parents, Sara and Gerald Murphy. She's the living continuation of the American social novel." This was just a normal direction from my father, like "Don't slouch at the dinner table." I want you to pay attention to this woman tonight because she is the living continuation of THE American social novel. Okay, Dad. "Dorothy Parker was her nanny. Played on the beach in Antibes with Picasso." All right, all right. I heard ya.

In addition to socializing with the local literati, my parents also hosted a number of friends from St. Louis that summer— ironic since the reason we'd come here in the first place was to escape the old routines. One of the first people to visit was my father's old friend Eileen Ellsworth, a divorcée with a six-year-old son, who came, too. Physically, Eileen was the exact opposite of my mother. Tall, brunette, olive-complected, leathery-looking. Like my mother, Eileen was a depressive. I never imagine tall people as prone to depression but she was that, a tall depressive. She was quick and theoretically funny. Her voice was deep and theatrical and I hated her. There wasn't a story my father could tell too many times as far as Eileen was concerned. "Oh, that is wonderful, Steve," she'd say, drying her eyes and fluffing her mane.

Even at seven I understood that my mother was fighting this woman for my father, one beguiling depressive battling it out with another for the affection of a novelist. Classic stuff, been going on since the beginning of time. I had no idea why a woman who threatened my mother so completely, a woman I was sure was his mistress, had come to the East End of Long Island to stay with us. But, as always, manners were important; you wouldn't want to offend your husband's lover by insinuating she wasn't welcome in your home.

At cocktail hour the night Eileen Ellsworth arrived, my mother was in a T-shirt and dungarees, as she called them, sitting with my father in the living room. Eileen came down the stairs in a silky blouse and slacks. My mother said something about getting cleaned up and a few minutes later came down the stairs in a sexy shirt and a denim skirt, little heels. Eileen then said something about realizing it was too humid for a silk shirt and a few minutes later came down once again, trying to be nonchalant, in a dress and heels and lipstick. My father simply complimented every entrance with equal weight. "Eileen, you're absolutely right. Let's celebrate your arrival and get dressed up. Doris, *che bella*!" My mother laughed and went back up and descended the stairs again and she might as well have been carrying a gun the fight was so over. She busted out her Diane von Furstenberg wrap dress, heels, coral lipstick, a little blue eye shadow. She had a sexy gap between her two front teeth, and she stuck out in all the right places, which seems even more impressive at five feet tall. Eileen Ellsworth and her son, Davey, went back to St. Louis a few days later. I never saw her again.

It seemed like when you made a break from the past, people wanted to be a part of it, often people from your past. After Eileen came Aunt Carol and Uncle Tom, just as we were preparing for Hurricane Belle, our first hurricane, possibly our last if we moved back to St. Louis when the year was up like we were supposed to. Our electricity was already gone. We got one TV channel out of Rhode Island and when that went out we listened to the radio for reports. Our phone went dead sometime during the morning bluster. We filled the bathtubs with water. We lit the tall green candles on the long wood dining table. A hurricane was no impediment to Mom and Dad's socializing. They got dressed up for Hurricane Belle. My mother put on a multicolored silk, floor-length muumuu— splashy orange, purple and pink, her hair in a short, late '70s salt-and-pepper perm, lots of jewelry. Dad put on an old top hat and tails of his father, Dagwood's.

My uncle Tom (not our real uncle, but our father's best friend) was dating my aunt Carol (my mother's half sister). These two couldn't have been a more unlikely couple. Tom was boozy, prone to break out in song at any moment or suddenly sit down and write a musical. He and my father had written a really funny election musical called *GUV!* and also a Watergate Christmas carol, and they did, in fact, with a few drinks under their belt, head out with a large group of drunken

St. Louis Democrats in 1972, and sing it door-to-door. But one carol no one ever expected Tom to take to the streets with was Aunt Carol. Uncle Tom had been drunk for days.

It wasn't just the alcoholics the storm was rattling; the animals were out of sorts as well. Our dog, Jubjub, ate my dad's nine-foot surf-casting rod, and one of the corgis belonging to the neighbor living in the icehouse next door ran off into the storm.

The dog's owner, Eleanor Ward, came by to see if it had taken shelter in our barn. Mom and Dad invited her in for a drink. I loved the way they got someone a drink as the response to any dilemma. So cinematic. Like a social doctor. I couldn't wait to say to someone who came to me with a serious problem, "My God, Jan, that's awful. Can I get you a drink?" or even better, "You look like you could use a drink."

Eleanor and Kate were sent out to look for the missing corgi. Through the rain and winds they searched the fields and the farm's dirt roads. When they returned, the little lost dog was inside playing with my sister Julia while Eleanor and Mom and Dad sang songs from *Candide* blaring on the stereo. Mom and Dad were good together, they looked great together, he was six-one with dark brown hair, she was five feet and blond, they were singy and dancy and funny, and it seemed to me during this storm that love was fun and costumed and gusty and uncertain.

Then, with a very limited amount of money that would have to last us an entire year in New York and with borrowing from Nonnie being an absolute impossibility, my mother joined the Devon Yacht Club shortly after we arrived. The Devon Yacht Club was the ramshackle alternative to the real country club in East Hampton, the Maidstone Club. Devon was on the sound, Maidstone was on the ocean. The Maidstone was a Tudor manse built in 1891. Devon was a cluster of crumbly old gray-and-white clapboard buildings that needed a paint job so badly that from out on the sound it looked like a coconut cake. The main building had dances every Thursday night. (For which Mom bought four . . . what can only be called gas station attendant jumpsuits—colorful oufits with stripes down the side that had little Pennzoil and Sunoco patches on the arms—for all of us to wear if we needed to pull a sophisticated gas station look together. Everyone got a different color. My gas station jumpsuit was white and blue.)

This was a signature move of my mother's, buying four of the same item in four different colors. With four of us being so close in age—my mother had four kids in five years, or two sets of Irish twins with a one-year break—this retail practice seemed reasonable to her. Eleanor was the oldest, then Katharine, then a year off, then Julia and then me.

My dad wasn't a country club kind of guy, but rumor had it that George Plimpton, who lived next door to Devon, had a Fourth of July rivalry with the club's fireworks display every year, which must have sounded fun and New Yorky to the St. Louisan in my dad, and isn't this why we came to New York? I mean, you can write a book in St. Louis. You cannot, on the other hand, have a gin and tonic with George Plimpton at Busch's Grove in Ladue. And he probably figured the club would get everybody out of the house during the day so Mom could type up his finished pages and he could write. My father was the most distracted writer working in America. If my sister Katharine and I put together a game of catch in the backyard with some old ratty mitts we'd found, he'd come out within minutes looking for a piece of the action.

"Give me that ball, Jean-Joe. Do either of you girls know who Dizzy Dean was?" and the game was brought to a standstill with a lively portrait of a Cardinals pitcher in the '30s. I threw the ball as hard as I could. I did not, nor did any of us girls, push the ball off our shoulders like a shot put or "throw like a girl." My father taught us curveballs from sliders, fastballs and screwballs. Later, during his boxing phase, we would learn jabs from hooks, how to throw a punch, turning your fist ever so slightly at the end of the extension, and basic footwork.

My father caught my wild throw. "Jean-Joe, your tactics are a hundred percent Dizzy Dean. 'The Diz,' they called him. He and his brother Daffy were part of a team during the Depression called the Gashouse Gang." He threw the baseball to Katharine. "They were the dirtiest, most low-down bunch of players—just terrific. Now, he first played for the Cards but later for the Browns, God, it must have been 1947—"

I don't ever remember him passing up going to the beach with all of us, even though he probably should have been doing some work. That summer my father cleared the beach twice in one week with shark spottings that turned out to be schools of fish. He ran up and down the beach, waving his arms, a maniac in yellow-and-green Lilly Pulitzer trunks, cupping his hands to his mouth to amplify the danger. "Shark! Out of the water! I mean now, God damn it!" he said as if the entire beach were made up of insolent daughters. It was the summer after *Jaws* came out. He hadn't seen *Jaws*, of course, but everyone else had, and that was the problem. It got to the point where if he came down to the kitchen asking who wanted to go ride the waves at the beach, he was teased and made to promise not to save anyone that day.

Days later you'd hear him on the phone to St. Louis talking about how he couldn't get any work done.

"Jesus, Hereford, you wanna know how the novel's coming? People wanting to play tennis in the middle of the afternoon and throw a ball around every five minutes and there hasn't been one goddamn night that we haven't been to somebody's house for cocktails."

At Devon we met Elise. She became Julia's and my best friend. She was a summer person, not a townie like us. She went to Dalton with Robert Redford's children. The closest thing we had come to a celebrity was seeing Stan Musial, Stan the Man, St. Louis Cards baseball great from the '40s and '50s, in the parking lot of my grandmother's church after mass. Stan Musial / Robert Redford. Not much of a match. Elise's father was a lawyer. They had a pool. To Julia and me, Elise was our George Plimpton, our idea of New York; she knew everybody. We weren't going to meet anyone like her in St. Louis: she was urbane.

Eleanor and Kate were in Junior Yacht, Julia and I were in Sandpipers, the younger kids at Devon. One day the Sandpipers all headed out on sailboats by ourselves. Elise and I and one other girl, Tracy, kept capsizing and were terrified. The motorboat that was meant to monitor new sailors, *The Terror*, was nowhere to be seen. Elise and I decided to swim back to shore, even though this meant breaking the cardinal rule of sailing, Never abandon your vessel. Elise and I were kicked out of Devon for abandoning our sailboat. I couldn't go sailing anymore and I couldn't go on the camping trip and I was banned from the Thursday dances for the remainder of the summer. I ended up playing a lot of tennis by myself, hitting balls against the old backboard on Stony Hill Farm, and strangely developed an incredible serve.

Since Elise had nothing to do either since getting kicked out, Julia and I spent days and days at Elise's house, eating all their cold cuts and their fancy ice cream, never once calling our mom and never receiving a single call checking up on us. Mrs. Fleming would explode when we made messes and left wet swimsuits everywhere (we never had suits with us and were always borrowing them). "I will not have it! I will not have it in my house!" she'd yell, storming through rooms, Georgette Klinger cold cream on her face, in her white, feathered slippers, to find the three of us. Inevitably she couldn't take it anymore and would call our mother to say it was really time for us to go home.

At Elise's house we played a game called The Weinhausers, in which a poor townie family named the Weinhausers

imposed themselves on this wealthy family. The Weinhausers
stayed with you and ate all your food and watched your TV
and would never leave. They complained a lot about the conditions, too, in their irritating, loud voices. "Your house is too
cold!" "You're out of mayonnaise again!" Until finally the rich
family would get fed up and attack the Weinhausers, evicting
them from their home.

"Get outta my house, you lousy Weinhausers!" and Julia
would throw me and Elise out the kitchen back door. We'd
rap on the windows to come back in.

"Scram! All of you!" Julia would scream at the window,
and we'd run off in case she'd called the police on us. Then
we'd switch roles.

When we got bored with The Weinhausers we began talking about going to bars. Not necessarily because we wanted to
drink or meet men, just because it seemed like the next logical
thing to do. And not just any bar, we wanted desperately to
go to Stephen Talkhouse. Stephen Talkhouse was a local bar;
sometimes there was music but mostly just regulars having
drinks and finding someone on the Island to have sex with
who they hadn't already screwed fourteen times. Elise's older
sister Sasha said we were too young to go to Stephen Talkhouse
but she would take us next year, when we were nine and ten.

DAD'S NOVEL DIDN'T SELL. It was rejected by two publishers, and that was that. Dad later said, "I didn't even think

of rewriting it. Rewriting was not playing the game like a gentleman."

In January, Nonnie died. My father gathered us on the long couch in the barn's high-ceilinged living room.

"Nonnie died. In Florida. Neallie is with her," my father said.

"Neallie died, too?" Eleanor asked.

"No, I mean Neallie is with Nonnie right now so she's not alone."

"But Nonnie's dead, so that means Neallie is alone." Katharine, future copy editor, said.

"Neallie is fine. And Mama's going to be fine, she's just very sad. We'll let her be alone for a while so she can call Aunt Ruth and Aunt Carol."

Mom cried for at least a whole day and a half, which was really terrifying for us girls. A couple days later we all went to St. Louis for the funeral at Annunziata. Mom was a disaster. At Nonnie's funeral Mom tried to get in the casket with Nonnie. We stayed at Nonnie's house for a week and then we all went back to Stony Hill Farm except my mother, who stayed behind to settle Nonnie's estate.

Nonnie's will apparently had a little twist: My mother would get Nonnie's house only if she moved all of us back to St. Louis and lived in it. She would not be allowed to sell it.

My grandmother loved puzzles, really any kind accompanied by a big bowl of salty potato chips would do, especially brainteasers and card games. She liked any kind of action. When my sisters and I would get out the Monopoly board, my grandmother would get her German on and get out her long ironing board and iron the money before the game could officially begin. My mother inherited her mother's love of puzzles in the form of crosswords, and Nonnie's turned out to be the Sunday *New York Times* of wills. Mom was furious that some of her inheritance was contingent upon moving back to St. Louis, but it probably also felt like rejoining the workforce. As a retired child equestrian she hadn't competed in years, but she honed her brain-twisting skills daily, at the kitchen table, with a pencil and an iced coffee.

Over the next six months Mom was going back and forth to St. Louis, eventually managing to get around a very tight legal document to sell Nonnie's house and get the rest of her inheritance as well. We were back in shoes and hollandaise sauce, but how this all went down we didn't know. Mom was an awfully swell-looking lady: doors didn't so much open for her as they did fall off the hinges. She returned to Long Island in Nonnie's fur coat, Nonnie's big blue Oldsmobile Regency. She was happy to have been able to crack at least the house clause of the Germanic will but she was also profoundly changed. Maybe it was guilt that she left her mother and then she died while we were away or a feeling that we had left her mother for a book that didn't even sell. But something besides my grandmother's life had ended for my mom, some playfulness, a lightness.

Mom and Dad were becoming increasingly uncomfortable with bohemian rural life; in those days no one lived out in the Hamptons during the winter if their ancestors weren't born there. No one from St. Louis came to visit Long Island in February, Elise's family stopped coming after Thanksgiving, everyone stopped coming out to Long Island after Thanksgiving.

The barn was drafty, the nearest hospital was Southampton, which was a half-hour's drive on Route 27, and I almost died of Rocky Mountain spotted fever. The way Mom told the story was that I was delirious and dying on the couch while Dad was reading the *New York Times*. He came across an article about Rocky Mountain spotted fever and my symptoms matched up, so Mom found a clinic nearby that she could take me to and ran me down there and the doctor said I had the highest fever they'd ever recorded and reassured my mother that if she had waited another two hours to bring me in I would have died. From this near-death experience I gleaned that reading the *New York Times* will save your life. Doctors, well, who knows how effective they are, but newspapers, newspapers can save your goddamn life. "Thank God your father was reading the *Times* this morning. You might have died."

My parents may have finally realized it was time to get out of the East End, though, when, the second year there, I was moved up to fourth grade halfway through third grade due to apparent intelligence. If the schools were so bad as to be skipping me ahead grades, we needed to get out of town and quick.

One year in New York turned into the Thomas Wolfe quote. We had now been in New York for two years with no plans to go home again to St. Louis anytime soon.

We did not crawl back to St. Louis penniless, on our hands and knees, as Nonnie had predicted. We did not see Nonnie "very soon," as she had said that day at the car. We did not return to St. Louis and live in her house when she died, as was her will. Mom was thinking about a job for Dad. We were moving to Westchester.

GIVE US THIS DAY OUR DAILY BOURGUIGNON

B RONXVILLE, NEW YORK, is a squalid little square mile in lower Westchester, twenty-eight minutes to midtown on the Metro-North, with a seedy downtown of Tudor flower shops and stores where pink corduroys for fathers can be purchased. Up near our house was a wasteland of country clubs and manses where lowlifes like the Kennedys once lived. As my dad put it, "People had some dough." But we were in our own little financial microclimate in the bullish Bronxville. We survived on the interest of the writer-proof trust fund that Nonnie had set up. (A mis-trust fund?) The interest we got every four months wasn't enough for a family of six people without eating disorders to live on. But this didn't seem to faze Mom and Dad. They bought a five-bedroom house, a shell our mother called it, in one of the most expensive towns in Westchester. Nothing was in tip-top condition—if rats bother you it might not suit your tastes—but everybody had her own room and it was in a new town where Dad hadn't told anyone to fuck off yet. Bronxville was chosen for its good public school, and my parents figured they could ignore the anti-Carter bumper stickers in exchange for this. The plan was that Dad was going to get a job, a real job, and he did.

His brief stint in the world of the Manhattan-bound 8:02 was as a speechwriter for William Paley, founder and chairman of CBS, for six months. My dad had an office at the CBS Black Rock building and worked regular hours. He got a little yellow Puch moped that he rode to the train station in his Brooks Brothers suits in the morning and left at the station to ride home at night, until one day some kids stole it and set it on fire.

When he was working for Paley he was boxing a night or two a week at Gleason's Gym near Madison Square Garden. He took lessons from this old trainer named Sammy Morgan who had trained a lot of good boxers, like welterweight Stanley "Baby" Sims in the '40s, and a Capuchin priest, and Miles Davis, who apparently was also a good boxer. My dad would bring Sammy back to Bronxville, surprising my mom with this old trainer with his gigantic beat-up boxer's nose and his smelly dogs. After dinner Dad would interview Sammy for a piece on boxing he was going to send to *The New Yorker.* My mother was happy during the yellow-moped year. Or the yellow-moped six months. It was the first time since my dad was a reporter at the *St. Louis Review* that he was out of the house.

We got a new dog, a Kerry blue terrier we named Guinness. This dog was supposed to be our new civilized dog, unlike Jubjub, our last dog in Amagansett and all the other criminally insane dogs we had owned who "had to go." Dogs would disappear one day and you'd ask, "Where's Jubjub?" and my mom would just say, "Oh, he had to go," as if he had a dentist appointment in midtown.

But Guinness was unrepentantly vicious. He scratched, bit, jumped on people, leaving trails of raised white flesh down your thighs. He murdered our bird, Oiseau. Neighborhood kids left our house looking like they'd been jumped—crying, with rips in their clothing, scratches on their legs and arms. When we had Mrs. Spaeth over to our new house for the first time, we were sitting in the living room having cocktails, trying to look presentable to the elderly art patron, when Guinness came into the room, his teeth gripping a used maxi pad he had dug out of the bathroom garbage. He sat on the white carpet next to Mrs. Spaeth gnawing on his bloody chew toy, until my dad managed to get it out of his mouth and hand it to my mother as Eloise talked about the Calder exhibit at the 1952 Venice Biennale.

In Bronxville we became devout twice-a-year Catholics, Christmas and Easter. My mother and father were tanked at every midnight mass and we were always late and my mother toddled into St. Joseph's Church in town in Nonnie's mink coat and demanded to sit in the front pew as if we were at a Broadway show. I don't think I once connected with a sermon. Who were those creepy bachelors who collected the baskets during mass? Did they have to look so sad while they took your money? I did love the "Peace be with you" part of mass, reaching out and shaking hands with people you didn't know, touching strangers and wishing them well. Shaking hands with that trembly old lady with the furry chin like a kiwi whose hands felt like little earthquakes. That was nice. Mom and Dad were too disorganized for more regular worship. There was never any talk of God or faith—odd, considering they had both gone to Catholic schools through college. As she smoked and read the paper in bed, Mom bragged about being certified to teach catechism, but when I came home one day and said, "I don't think I believe God is real," she just said, "All right, sweet pea. Let's see what Half Pint is up to, shall we?" and we snuck a *Little House on the Prairie* rerun before Dad came home. It seemed as if everything they once valued, everything important, we had given up. St. Louis, our hometown, gone. The Catholic Church, an awful lot of effort. Family, no extended family around at all. On Long Island we had been untethered, but we'd had a deadline, for the book, of one year, and then we were going back to all the things we had known. Now there was no going back to who we had been. We were all trying out new ideas of who or what we were going to be in Westchester.

I was the baby.

One mile from home in Jelly-bean town,
Lives Jeanne, the Jelly-bean Queen.
She loves her dice and treats 'em nice;
No dice would treat her mean.

Her Jelly Roll can twist your soul
Her eyes are big and brown,

She's the Queen of the Queens of the Jelly-beans—
My Jeanne of Jelly-bean Town.

Dad would often say-sing this bit from F. Scott Fitzgerald's short story "The Jelly-Bean" as he tucked me in at night, past the age when others had been tucked in, for which I took a lot of shit from my sisters. They thought it was babyish to still be tucked in at ten years old and it was, but this is when I got his full attention and stories of his childhood in St. Louis.

For a long time I thought Dad had written "The Jelly-Bean" about me. He was a writer. My name was Jeanne. The name in the poem was spelled how I spelled Jeanne, the French spelling of Jean (pronounced Jeannie), so it must have been written by Dad for me. I never questioned the brown eyes in it and the fact that mine are blue. "The Jelly-Bean," not that I understood a word of it at the time, is about Jim Powell, a jelly bean, a southern term for an idler. Jim's family was once prominent, but after his parents die, he's alone, the house gets sold, and he is no longer part of Georgia society. He's back in town after a stint in the Navy during the war, and he gets invited to a country club dance—the kind of fancy affair he doesn't normally hang around, and he meets a gorgeous society girl named Nancy Lamar with a thing for highballs. Jim falls in love with her, but the next day hears that after he left her the night before at the dance, she ran off and married some other guy. The woman is, yes, like Zelda Fitzgerald but also like Mom at that age. Her wildness and beauty are what captivate Jim, not anything like kindness or intelligence. And like Jim Powell, Dad was in the Navy and had come from a prominent family.

As he tucked me in, Dad told me stories about Ella Voss, his black nanny, who had been emancipated at age eight in 1863 in Helena, Arkansas, and had come to be his mother's nanny, and then, when she had children, Ella took care of my father and his brother and three sisters, too. He lovingly imitated Ella Voss and her baffling refrain for any situation he brought to her as a young boy: "Lye rose catch medlars, Mister Steve, lye rose catch medlars." He wasn't sure what this actually meant, but it came to be comforting, even in its mysteriousness. If any of the five children spilled their milk at the dinner table they'd be sent into the kitchen to eat with the help. My father would intentionally spill his milk to eat with Ella Voss and her sisters Ginny, Alberta, and Odessa, who also helped out at their house, and hear stories of their lives.

My father said his mother gave birth to him and had a Corona typewriter on her lap a couple hours later to finish her daily column, "Here and There," for the *St. Louis Globe-Democrat*. "Ella was all I knew, raised me, and then one day when I was about six this white woman comes in and says she's my mother. My sister Tad cried when she found out she was white. Just fell apart." My father, a man who has gone through life with just half a degree of separation, told me that Grandma Darst had, for about fifteen minutes, until she decided it was complete silliness, been in the UDC, United Daughters of the Confederacy, with Tennessee Williams's mother. His sister Betty was friendly with Dakin Williams, Tennessee's brother.

His childhood was teeming with characters and artists and newspaper life and kids and race relations, politics, civil rights and funny stories. It sounded crazy and wonderful, and yet I knew listening to him that there was something else at work. My father's stories were postdated checks, promissory notes of what was to be restored: the prominence, the name, the black chauffeurs smoking and having a plate of food at the back door of their house on Westminster Place while his uncle Joe, the mayor of St. Louis, was inside talking with his mother and father about housing for the poor, civil rights, revitalizing the city economically, the plans for the Saarinen arch on the riverfront. They were meant to sustain us, sustain him, until a better day, a day when he would fulfill his promise as a writer. It didn't take a lot of convincing to get Dad to tell stories about his childhood, St. Louis or his family. The past was his number-one love. If there is some genetic opposite of my father it might be Madonna. I wonder if reinventing yourself would even be a concept that my father could grasp. Reinvent? My father didn't even rewrite.

I was heading unenthusiastically into the fifth grade. I thought having skipped a grade out in Amagansett proved that I had already conquered school. I didn't want to be a writer, I wanted to be a detective. I carried a huge satchel around with me wherever I went, even just around the house. There was an office in this bag: pens, yellow lined legal pads stolen from Dad, a camera, a tape recorder, baby powder for fingerprinting, handcuffs. Others in the family didn't see my potential as a private eye, however, they just saw me as a dick. It seemed that if I touched something, it broke; if I borrowed a sweater from one of my sisters, a scoop of chocolate ice cream would catapult itself off my cone onto my chest; if Eleanor and Julia were piling on Katharine, joking around, I'd join in, throwing my weight on the pile, but for some reason my jump would be the one that would bust Katharine's wrist. I don't know if you've ever been accused of being an imbecile, but if you have, you know that once word has gotten out that you are a moron, there is no turning public opinion back in your favor.

"What is wrong with you?" My mother had said these words so many times to me that my sisters had adopted them. I had a habit of grabbing some scissors and pulling up a chair while my mother cooked dinner. I cut up whatever was in sight—letters, bills, report cards—it was relaxing after a long day at school to just cut things up, cut, cut, cut. The way some people needlepoint. My father saw me doing this once and said, "Don't be an idiot." I didn't speak to him all night, and then I wrote a retaliatory note to him, in pencil so dark it ripped the paper. I pressed down on it like a dying man, writing, "I am not an idiote. Do not call me one!" I put it on his pillow. My dad apologized right away but from that day on whenever I did something stupid, my sisters would say, "I am not an ID-I-OTE! Do not call me one!" in the voice of John Merrick, the Elephant Man.

My sisters and I were the Marx Brothers for Halloween for four years in a row. Eleanor was Groucho, Katharine was Chico, Julia was Harpo, and I was Zeppo. Remember Zeppo?

Of course you don't, nobody remembers Zeppo, because he was the "unknown" Marx brother, the normal one, the straight man. Zeppo. Who knew what Zeppo even looked like. I could have worn a kilt and carried bagpipes, for all anybody knew about this brother. This is the essence of being the youngest kid. In exchange for shabby treatment, however, comes the dubious reward of incompetence. I was someone with no responsibilities. I'd be putting a cup in the dishwasher when Eleanor or Katharine would snatch it out of my hand.

"Mom! Jeanne was trying to put a mug in the dishwasher! You should have seen her!" Did I have no responsibilities because I was an imbecile or was I an imbecile because I had no responsibilities?

Julia was developing a love of paperwork and red tape. She was a sort of child notary public; if you asked to borrow her baseball mitt, she would quickly draw up a lot of forms for you to sign and date, with a lot of dramatic stamping on these forms, and then she'd say, "I'll have my people look into this and get back to you." Just for kicks she'd sit and copy the Bible onto yellow legal pads.

She set up a real estate office in the basement with files of available properties on index cards. The problem was no one ever went down in the basement, it wasn't renovated or anything, it was like the basement of an apartment building, complete with boiler and cement floors, cold, musty, dark.

After a while she'd come up to the kitchen and make an announcement.

"Ah, good morning, everyone. I'd like to let all you people know that my office is now open for business and I've got some terrific new properties you really should have a look at. A very airy condo in Boca Raton, right on the beach. Excellent price. Stop by, I'd be happy to go over the details with any of you." And she'd head downstairs for a few hours.

The only family members Julia liked to talk to were Guinness and Oiseau and our cat. Yes, Julia talked to the animals, and sometimes renamed them; Guinness became Toddy, after Hot Toddy, a delightful concoction of whiskey, sugar and lemon that we had discovered and fallen in love with when a nasty flu was going around. Our cat, Kitty, became Cuckoo. Of course, no one used these new names but Julia.

"Cuckoo doesn't like it when you smoke at the table, Mother," Julia would announce at dinner, and we'd all think, "Who the fuck is Cuckoo?"

She also spent a lot of nights at her librarian's station in the living room, where she checked out books. If you were just passing through the living room she would attempt to lure you into the library.

"Excuse me, ma'am? Can I interest you in a book today? Perhaps Freud's *Dora: An Analysis of a Case of Hysteria*? No? Well, then, let's see what else we have here . . . What about this wonderful biography of Matisse, you look like an art lover," she'd say, letting out a loud cackle.

Julia would copy the Bible while I checked out *Tales of the Jazz Age,* which contained "The Jelly-Bean," and we'd sit in her "library," where she had pulled a table into the middle of the room to create a checkout desk, silent but together in our two pretend worlds.

KATHARINE WAS THE READER of all of us. Reading was more like a compulsion than a pastime with her, like a bowl of nuts on the table. If there was something, anything, between you and Katharine—Hemingway, a phone bill—she must, must pick it up and read it. If she was ever to visit you on death row with those little cubicles and Plexiglas dividers, I sure as hell hope no one left behind a *People* magazine on the table. "Umm hmm. So what time is the execu—Whoa! Look at how fat Alec Baldwin's gotten!"

I was more of a periodic, occasionally-falling-in-to-a-book-I-just-couldn't-find-my-way-out-of reader, but Katharine was a daily reader. She didn't read to please Dad; she was just a genuinely passionate reader.

She read while doing other things, multitasking back when it was called rudeness. Since our father forbade any activity during dinner other than conversation—no music, no reading, and definitely no television—my sister would pick up ketchup bottles or turn over a fork to read the inscription on the back of it.

She was the good kid of all of us, the good student, the friend to us all. She remains the only person on speaking terms with everyone, the rest of us have a speaking-to percentage of about forty-five. While Eleanor, Julia and I were ripping each other's arms off while going in for the last bunch of asparagus slathered in hollandaise, Katharine was bringing the empty platter into the kitchen on the philanthropic errand of fetching more. Once in the kitchen, she fell into the expectant pages of a Craig Claiborne cookbook on the table until my mother would call for her and the remaining asparagus. Some people can't live in the moment. Katharine couldn't get out of the moment.

She read while you were reading to her. I'd stand in her bedroom doorway reading her the part in *The Crucible* where Giles Corey defends himself from Thomas Putnam's witchy accusations with "A fart on Thomas Putnam!" which filled me with hope that good literature and fart jokes were not mutually exclusive, until I realized she was dropping her eyes down to a copy of *Pride and Prejudice* balanced on her stomach—a book that could have used a little farting to liven it up, in my opinion.

She loved the book as object. I remember the shame I felt, more than once, when Katharine caught me placing a book on its spine or dog-earing pages. "Jeanne, you can't do that to books! Look what you did," and she would pick up the victimized text, hold it up for me to consider its plight. "You can't treat books this way!" she would say, as if you had just stubbed out your cigarette between Lassie's eyes.

Even though she chose reading over a word or two with me time and time again, I wanted to be her confidante in a way that knows no discouragement. She had something I did not, an escape hatch, and I wanted her to show it to me.

AS THE OLDEST, Eleanor always had to take care of us and it seemed like from a very early age, Eleanor did not want to be like Mom and Dad in any way. When Mom became a serious cook in Bronxville, Eleanor had to have a dinner different from what everyone else was having, as if she were a VIP ordering off the menu. "I'll have a cube steak, Mom." Always the same thing. Cube steak and a chunk of iceberg lettuce with Green Goddess dressing. She loved any kind of convenience food, preferred it to fresh food. She thought we were all awfully silly with our roasted potatoes and rosemary roast chicken. If the packaged version of some food was available, she'd always choose that over its natural state and eat it as if it was just the most luxurious thing in the world. Eleanor was a theater person at Bronxville High School, but her real love was television. She defied Dad by being blatantly middlebrow. She did not even pretend to care about books. She'd simply say, "I don't like reading unless I have to," or something equally mind-blowing to my father. If she could have gotten away with it she might have said, "Dad, I don't care about books anymore. I'm on to new stuff now. The whole world's on to new stuff now."

One night, shortly after we had moved to Bronxville, my parents went out to dinner in the city and Eleanor, as usual, was in charge of everybody. She heated up some pot pies and announced we would be watching *The Ordeal of Patty Hearst* on TV.

Katharine was on the divan and Julia and Eleanor and I were all on the carpet, leaning against Mom and Dad's bed. Guinness was at the top of the stairs behind the door that led downstairs. Guinness barked quite a bit, but the main thing that provoked barking and violent attacks was not the sound of intruders or other dogs on the street but the sound of laughter. Nothing made our dog more nuts than the sound of people enjoying themselves, but in particular it was Katharine's laugh that drove Guinness to attack. When he heard Katharine laugh, Guinness would charge Katharine and maul her. I can understand the impulse, certainly; some people's laughs make me want to attack in the same way. Too-loud laughs—too fake—a combination of too loud AND fake, in abundance in Southern California and on television, are bite-worthy. But Katharine's laugh is just an ordinary ha-HA! kind of laugh, ever so slightly higher in pitch than her normal voice. Which was why it was so continually surprising that he should single her out. When she would laugh in the kitchen, where Guinness dwelt most of the time, you'd just glare at her as if to say "What the fuck are you doing?" and then, as if Katharine had stuck a steak in her shirt, Guinness would run at her and bite her legs, jump on her, scratch her legs with his claws, nip at her arms, all the while barking and growling.

At one point in *The Ordeal of Patty Hearst*, I got up to go to the bathroom. I thought it was odd when I returned that no one had taken my seat, because it was a desired front-of-TV kind of spot and in a house of four girls, nothing was still yours if you walked away from it. So maybe I should have known something sinister was under way. The movie ended. Eleanor got up, walked to the TV and shut it off, something I had never seen her do without having Dad tell her to. She turned and looked at me.

"You're Patty Hearst and we're the SLA."

"What?" I said. I wasn't even a brunette. Who was casting this kidnapping?

Katharine and Julia went and stood next to Eleanor in a police-barricade formation.

"We're the SLA. Now get on your feet." It could be hours before Mom and Dad got home.

I scrambled to my feet and tried to ram my head through them to get out of my parents' bedroom but they pushed me to the floor and kneed my face into the carpet.

"Who's got the rope?" Eleanor yelled.

Julia held one over her head. "Affirmativo!"

Eleanor grabbed the rope and as I wriggled and squirmed Eleanor and her two goons managed to hog-tie me and then blindfold me with a scarf of Mom's. Next they got me on their shoulders and began carrying me down the front stairs and into the kitchen where Guinness became part of the procession, barking and jumping up at my stomach. After nearly dropping me several times they finally headed back up the front stairs and opened a linen closet and threw me in. Guinness leapt into the closet with me and that's when the SLA shut the door. Guinness proceeded to scratch my legs and arms and bark wildly. I yelled and yelled but it was no use. I wasn't sure whether I would be getting out in a few minutes or when my parents got home. I heard laughter and talking above the barking but no specifics of my fate. The darkness of the closet was really riling Guinness up. I don't know how long I was in there with that terrier but at some point I heard the front door slam and I prayed it was my drunken parents.

"Goils?" I heard my dad call up the stairs. Guinness began barking like crazy again.

My father opened the closet door and untied me. My mother came up the stairs.

"Oh, for heaven's sake. Is that my scarf? Girls?" My captors emerged from their rooms.

Eleanor and Katharine explained the game.

My father said, "Are you still our Patty?"

I gave him a look of death.

"You haven't turned into Tania yet?"

"No, Dad," I said, rubbing my red thighs, which were burning with white, raised claw marks.

My dad patted his jacket pocket looking for his glasses to inspect my wounds. He was always looking for his glasses the way drinkers are forever trying to remember where they set their drink down.

"We'll look at those scratches in the morning. Good night, goils," he said.

———

So, from oldest to youngest we had: a book-hater, a compulsive reader, a paperwork fanatic and an idiot detective.

MOM'S NEW BRONXVILLE PERSONA was about normalcy. She was embarking on a brand-new personal adventure of dullness. Watch me as I transform into the biggest suburban dud mom you've ever seen. Being a normal mom involved one pottery class in White Plains, and later one single aerobics class at the school gym. I'm happy to say she never donned leg warmers or a bodysuit. Her jogging career spanned two separate jogs with me around the neighborhood with frequent cig breaks. That was it for her involvement in public life. No clubs, classes, exercise, lunches. No PTA commitments or Junior League or friends. My mother hung out in the kitchen all day long. No one bugging her too much, her days spent at the long butcher-block table, smoking, doing the *New York Times* crossword, making herself iced teas and little cold steak sandwiches with ketchup, occasionally driving down to the Bronxville Police Department, which had built a brand-new doggy jail because Guinness kept getting out of our house and terrorizing people and eventually mauling an old woman's toy poodle to death. After springing Guinness she might watch a little tennis on the small TV, but otherwise she'd flip through cookbooks, make grocery lists, feed Oiseau. She'd talk to whatever visitors came through, her kids, their friends, sign a report card or two. The only thing Mom read was the newspaper, period. She conceived of meals and went to the grocery store and cooked. This was the new Mom.

Her repertoire, Northern Italian and French mixed with midwestern basics, might have been called Mussolini in Missouri or Mid-*Ouest* Boozer. She made classic midwestern stuff like lamb with mint jelly, German potato salad, ham steak with applesauce, the world's greatest fried chicken. From our time living in Amagansett she'd picked up more rustic coastal summer dishes like mussels in white wine and garlic, fried trout with cucumber-dill sauce, duck à l'orange, broiled tomatoes (bread crumbs, olive oil and garlic on top, usually served with steak), and things she threw on a fire like roasted onions cooked and served in tinfoil with tons of butter and salt (so simple, and I don't know anyone else who makes onions like this). A regular weeknight dinner might be coq au vin, veal marsala or chicken cacciatore. She liked a challenge, making things like, on occasion, pot-au-feu, which she pronounced *pot-uh-fooooo*. People who say there's nothing worse than "a little knowledge" have never experienced my mother's "a little French." She mispronounced everything: *un* was *ume*, *un peu* was *ume pooo*, *bon appétit* was *bone appetitaaah*. Over-the-top incorrect, but she was convinced her accent was "divine." She and my father went through a homemade-pasta phase in the early '80s, using a chrome pasta maker that attached to the butcher-block table. My dad made the pasta: shaping a pile of flour on the table and cracking an egg into it and pushing the dough through the machine rollers to flatten it and then guiding the eggy mass through the chrome teeth while they drank wine, blared *The Marriage of Figaro*, and Mom made her spaghetti sauce with beef and vegetables. She made incredible spinach cannelloni with Dad's flat lasagna-like noodles. She made a salad where she cooked up some bacon, saved the grease and mixed it with red wine vinegar and sugar and whisked it together and drizzled it on romaine lettuce with the bacon. It was insanely good. She made her own mayonnaise with herbs like tarragon and basil that made her chicken salad sandwiches fantastic. She didn't overvalue cleanliness in her kitchen; Guinness frequently jumped up, twisted his neck sideways and licked the side of the butter while my mother worked away. I wouldn't be surprised if we ate more than a few cigarette ashes in our lifetime. Butter and salt were practically rubbed on her own children before she'd give us a kiss hello. But the way she made anything was simply tastier than anyone else. I've never had buttered toast as good as hers.

DAD NOW WORE A SUIT to work every day, but I never got the feeling he was "new Dad" to go along with our new house, new dog, new town. He was definitely old dad. I never got the sense that he saw taking the train in every morning as anything other than another experience, like research. He didn't seem like anyone else's dad, in it, the grind, the rat race, for the long haul. His mind was always on the thing he'd rather be doing, writing. On weekends he took notes and worked on ideas and followed hunches.

"Who's up for a drive?" Considering the amount of carbon monoxide involved in going anywhere farther than town in our car, no one was ever up for a drive in our family. Eyes, mouths all contorted into polite interest mode. "I thought we'd head out to Sands Point and check out the real Gatsby mansion." The idea flopped big-time: No one wanted to go look at some dumb house and get a school-like lecture. But somebody had to go with the guy; you can't just let a man head off alone looking for a fictional town called East Egg, so I said I would go.

It started to rain the minute the car got on the Hutchinson River Parkway. A little radio might have been nice but Dad didn't allow anything but low jazz underneath his conversation, so I just stared ahead at the highway.

"This is gonna be terrific, Jean-Joe, I'm glad you came along. What the hell is wrong with those girls? They're gonna be bedridden with regret when they find out what they missed out on. So what are you reading?"

"Ummm. *From the Mixed-up Files of Mrs. Basil E. Frankweiler.*"

"Don't know it. Now, when do they read *The Great Gatsby* in school these days?"

"I'm not sure."

"Well, I'll try and find out. I hope to hell they don't waste a lot of time on Salinger."

We got to the house in a little over an hour. We parked the car on the side of the road. It was now a total downpour. I didn't have a rain jacket. We got out of the car and walked a bit. Dad had on his gray felt fedora, which he plunked on my head. "Now, this house here," he said, as we stood in front of a gate-house and a large gate with tall hedges on either side, "used to be the home of a Mrs. Belmont, a suffragette. Later bought by Hearst but he left it to go run his papers in the West and be with Marion Davies. Absolute monstrosity, torn down in 1940. It's possible Fitzgerald was here, but this isn't the Gatsby house."

"It's torn down?" I asked. He had said nothing of going to see a house that wasn't in fact there anymore.

He started walking down the street. I followed.

I pushed the big hat back on my head and wiped the rain from my face. We crossed the road and walked back toward the death mobile. I wiped my eyes again, waiting for something to happen.

"Most people think it was the Swope house not too far from here, but Fitzgerald was never at that house, he visited a different house of theirs. I'm going to hit the Great Neck library next weekend, have a look at the Great Neck newspapers. I have got a few hunches about some people Fitzgerald based his characters on.

I nodded. I was freezing and hungry.

"All right. Let's head home, shall we, Jean-Joe?"

This new life Mom envisioned, the one she paid for, the Westchester us, normal and fancy, didn't last long. When the CBS job ended Dad began talking about not another job but another novel.

THE CHICKEN SALAD
FINANCIAL INDEX

WITH THE JOB at CBS over, Dad was fleshing out the idea for a second novel, called *Black Ink*, inspired by his time at CBS, about the owner of a TV network.

"It's done in a Waugh style. The network (like CBS) likes to hire celebrities, and the narrator is there to represent Catholics—he's written for a Catholic publication, very liberal—and is advised that working for the hawkish network will be just like that but that it might be a little more difficult typing with blood on his hands, otherwise okay. His name is Francis F. X. Xavier, descendant on both sides of the number-two man in the founding of the Jesuits, Francis Xavier, for whom many, many Catholics are named."

My mother preferred his flesh out on Fifty-second Street. This was not the direction she wanted to be going in.

I now went to school all the time with no lunch money. I would ask my dad for a dollar and sometimes he'd go to his dresser and take change off of it and sometimes he would just say he didn't have it. You'll be fine, he seemed to say, opening the front door for me. Go read, go listen, go ask questions about what you're learning. Lunch will come. Lunch isn't why you go to school.

What I was taught about money from my father was that scraping through life builds character, that driving around in our fume-spewing 1971 Ford Torino wagon while other people had new BMWs with red bows on the front in their driveways on Christmas morning made us more interesting than other people, and of course, that money destroys creativity. And last, the very solid: Money doesn't make you happy.

After hustling up some lunch for myself at school, an apple here, a muffin someone didn't want there, I'd come home ravenous and find my mother in her office, the butcher-block kitchen table. "Never spend your capital, baby" was one afternoon's money lesson from her. At the kitchen table you would also hear gems such as: "It's just as easy to fall in love with a rich man as a poor man." And then there was her signature, "Money doesn't make you *un*happy, you know." This was the extent of the financial workings of the world as far as I knew. I was never taught how to balance a checkbook or how credit cards worked. (All I knew was that my mom's worked, my father's didn't.) We had a conversation once about economics and we were talking about other parts of the country.

"What about Maine?" she said, puffing on her cigarette. "Now, that's poverty. A chicken salad sandwich there is only about three dollars!"

I call this my mother's Chicken Salad Financial Index.

———————

WE DIDN'T HAVE health insurance. We knew not to break anything, not to swallow anything other than food, not to fall off anything or trip, not to let anything bite us unless it was our dog. The hot water was shut off all the time. I washed my hair on the third floor in Eleanor's claw-footed tub, which I could lean over and only my head would suffer the freezing water, and then my hair froze on the way to school because there was no heat in our car and it was twenty degrees outside so I had these popsicle locks. I could see my breath in my room in the winter. When things broke, like the shower in the front bathroom on the second floor, we just stopped using them. When our back steps rotted through, someone deemed the front door the only entrance worth using. The Torino wagon was now so rusted through that you could see the road from a hole in the backseat floor, there was a grease spot on the upholstery on the driver's side where my dad's head would touch it, and the gray fume puffs that came out of the tailpipe just needed some dialogue in them to be highly toxic cartoons. The Death Mobile, we called it.

MOM HOCKED THINGS from time to time. I remember later on in high school she passed my boyfriend the green beans almondine at our dinner table and asked, "Now, Martin, dear, do you know anyone who might want to buy a pair of antique revolvers? Darling little guns, they were Daddy's." I guess she figured if he was hanging around the high school at twenty-two looking for a girlfriend he might be the kind of person who might also know where to sell some guns.

Mom was seriously on Dad's case at this point. We needed food, clothes, ballroom-dance lessons. When something came up, my mother would raid the attic even though none of her things would fit any of us. The things in the trunks and boxes were seemingly from another culture entirely, like the mink stoles of Nonnie's with the heads still on. The idea that women wore small animal heads around their shoulders to indicate status and superiority over non–animal-head-wearing women, women who couldn't afford those little beady-eyed heads, was fascinating and nuts to me. The teeny bejeweled cat's-eyes glasses with double thick lenses that Mom wore from about the age of six on were so small that the four of us could never wear them even if we happened to go blind. The white gloves were for the smallest hands imaginable, the hands of a toddler it seemed to us. None of us standard human-sized girls could wear these things that Mom once wore to cotillions and balls. Not the velvet-covered black riding hats—not the teeny beige chaps, not the teeny-tiny riding blazers.

In those days it was weird if your father was around all day; this was before flex-time and perma-lancers and job-sharing. You either had a job or you didn't. I remember filling out

forms for the Girl Scouts and coming upon "Father's occupa-
tion: _____."

"What should I say Dad does?" I called out to my mother.

"Freelance writer," she'd yell and then mumble something
under her breath. It was always a moment-by-moment call,
what my father did. If he and my mother were getting along,
he was a writer. If they were fighting, my mom might yell,
"Absolutely nothing," to my question. Being a writer was like
being a baby in an Edward Albee play. Some days your writing
existed, some days it didn't, depending on how much people
had had to drink, if you had been flirting with some professor
down at Sarah Lawrence, if the car had died again and there
was no money to fix it.

I remember being mortified when walking with some kids
after school and seeing my dad coming out of the pretty red
brick house that was the Bronxville library. Other people's
fathers spent the day with people, not microfiche.

"Freelance writer." Surely my parents made this term up to
define the hanging around my father did most days? Friends'
parents seemed confused when I'd say "freelance writer," and
I'd think, Drop it. Just drop it.

"Who does he write for?"

"Himself," I would say.

"Oh, really! Anything I might have read?"

"Umm . . . not his novel, that wasn't published . . . do you
read *Harper's* magazine? . . . or *Commonweal*? It's a small Catholic magazine, very well regarded . . . he's in *The Norton Reader*,
too . . . what's *The Norton Reader*? It's um, an anthology . . ."

It was a real pain in the ass having a writer for a dad in a town that wasn't a haven for struggling artists or struggling anything. I heard Don DeLillo lived in Bronxville but I never saw his ass.

The people who did understand what freelance writer meant were my English teachers, a lot of whom were female, single, struggling writers who lived on the Upper West Side. To them, my dad was a gentleman artiste, someone maybe luckier than they as he didn't have to teach, someone who was living it, baby. Dad was asked by my tenth-grade English teacher to come and teach a writing class. He came in a suit, of course—my dad wears a suit, and often a hat, to the coffeemaker. He read the story in the Bible, John 11:35, where a bereft Jesus goes to his friend Lazarus's tomb and demands the stone from his tomb be removed and orders Lazarus out. My father read the shortest phrase in the Bible from that story. "Jesus wept," my father said, as his audience grew groggy.

"Don't ya just love that? Beautiful. It can't be improved upon. If you can get your writing down to just what's essential and then knock off five more words, you've got it. 'Jesus wept.' Now, raise your hand if you've read any Joyce at all and I mean even just opened it up and took a shot at it when you were feeling brave."

No hands were raised.

"Nothing to be embarrassed about, believe me. When the time's right you'll know. Now, the thing about Joyce . . ." The simplicity lesson my father was teaching then moved into Joyce and *The Dubliners*, T. S. Eliot's "The Waste Land,"

Proust, and a few English poets. I couldn't really follow it and it seemed like other students were equally perplexed. Unlike at home, though, my father was cut off abruptly after forty minutes by a loud bell that sent children flying past him like preppy pigeons muttering niceties. "Thanks for coming to our class, Mr. Darst." "Thanks for the writing lesson, have a nice weekend."

HE NEVER GOT ANOTHER regular job despite my mother's pleading, despite her feeling that he could get a teaching job—college, presumably, my father wouldn't go any lower than that. But teaching, on any level, it seemed, was completely out of the question as far as my dad was concerned.

When he wasn't at the Bronxville library he was up in his office on the third floor, a stuffy garret that my six-foot, one-inch father had to stoop over to enter. It wasn't a room, it was an unheated attic most of which served as stole storage, but after passing the Doris Gissy Museum of Ridiculous Fancy Childhoods, you entered a small open space that he had made into an office. There was nothing hanging on the walls, no carpet, no material comforts of any kind—just a giant desk, a giant desk chair, huge filing cabinets, his gray metal lamp with the ON button that you had to hold down until the long fluorescent bulb flickered like lightning as it came to life, pieces of paper with notes on them taped to walls, his microcassette recorder always within reach ("Note to self: Ah, reread

Kempton's latest *New York Review of Books* piece, terrific, just terrific"), a heavy magnifying glass, dictionaries everywhere that seemed to be mating and spawning baby dictionaries. It was appealing, if not entirely clear to me what went on in there. His gray filing cabinets, about the same height as me, were filled with his files, his writing, his ideas, notes on pieces to write, and also four files on each of us girls filled with report cards, pictures, notes we had written him or drawings we had made him. He seemed to be enjoying himself very much in his office even as other people seemed to be very, very angry with him. I saw my dad as a wanted man, a right-brain outlaw, with the authorities closing in on him.

HE WAS NOT JUST AROUND, he was available. Constantly. Positively up for chitchat, lots of it. With anyone.

"I was talking to the checkout girl at the A&P. Turns out her grandfather was in the Battle of Saint-Mihiel. Probably knew Dagwood."

"The checkout girl? How'd you get on that subject?" my mother asked.

"Oh, we were just chatting, you know. Hell of a nice gal."

After picking me up from Teen Center on a Friday night in the Death Mobile he would turn to the backseat and bellow to my friend, "Now, Shannon, who would you say, and I know it's tough to name just one, but if someone had a gun to your head, who would you say is your favorite essayist?"

Any transaction at all was a big one. Even answering the door on Halloween, a fairly mechanical interaction after a while, was alive with conversational possibilities.

"Well now, Charlie Chaplin, what have you got?"

"Dad, they don't have anything, just give them some candy," I would plead.

"Oh, come now. You've got to do something for this Baby Ruth! Do you think I'm going to simply unhand this chocolate bar for looks alone? Now, what about a poem? A joke? A song? Some verse?"

The kids would sheepishly start back down our walkway, mumbling to themselves.

"Jabberwocky? How about Who's on First?" my father would call at their backs.

AS FAR AS EMPLOYMENT, my mother, a woman who grew up with live-in horse trainers and kept a copy of the *Social Register* handy on our living room shelves should someone want to know who in the hell we were, wasn't about to go out and be somebody's receptionist at a dental office in town. (Which is just what she ended up doing.) She was increasingly pissed about supporting us, not something women who went to Manhattanville in 1959 routinely did. "I didn't sign up for this, sweetheart," she'd say to me as she warmed up for her nightly weepathon. The first mother I saw like mine was Amanda Wingfield in *The Glass Menagerie*, going into reveries about her suitors. There was Rodney, the man my mother should have married, she could have had lunch every day at the St. Louis Country Club. He was presumably a bore and a penny loafer guy. And was named Rodney. Or Chip Boulard, whose family owned the biggest lead company in the world. She could have had the fanciest pencils in all the world, I guess, which, when you're a crossword fanatic as she was, might be no small thing. She talked about how her father never said he loved her, how he worked all the time, how she never saw him, how her parents had a loveless marriage. She told stories of her structured childhood and her academic drive. I spoke French in preschool and now look at me, she seemed to say on a nightly basis.

WHILE MY FATHER'S PARENTS were pretty darn sparkly in their heyday, writing for newspapers and hosting radio shows, Katharine in particular being a well-known St. Louis columnist with a searing wit, they were not immune to the difficulties of the writing life, the ups and downs, the financial bumpiness, and when Dagwood died, Katharine's Chicken Salad Financial Index plummeted. Her driver, Edward, came up with the idea of picking her up at the paper, driving her home, opening the car door for her and then, as she made her way up the front walk, transforming superhero style into the butler. As Katharine approached the front door, Edward would dash around to the side door, throw off his chauffeur jacket, throw on a white coat for serving, and rush through the interior of the house to answer the front door for her, as if he were now an entirely different person, and ask her if she wanted her usual martini. Much later, in her seventies, she got by with small writing gigs people gave her. "Crazy Kate," as her five kids called her, lived out the remainder of her life rather meagerly in a crummy apartment building in St. Louis, with no comforts or financial security, until she went totally mad and lived until her death with my aunt Betty and her eight kids in Betty's turn-of-the-century mansion—which had a working elevator but a nonworking front door, so for years people entered through a gigantic first-floor window.

Writing seemed to get rather rough in your later years. This was the side I was aware of as a kid—the curse of the writing life, the way it seemed to leave you in a tough spot in your old age. I didn't see lawyers suffering like this in their later years. And I worried that my dad might be headed down the same road as his mother. When I read *Death of a Salesman,* I saw my father so clearly in Willy Loman, clinging just a little too tightly to some importance he had known in St. Louis to keep himself going, peddling graphs no one wanted. Knowing that we had no health insurance, let alone life insurance to cash out like Willy, helped me sleep at night. My father's slipping grip on his dream showed itself in various ways. He insisted you look at him while he talked. If you dropped your fork at dinner and your eyes dropped to locate it while he was theorizing on "The Waste Land," he'd bark, "Look at me while I'm talking to you, God damn it." You'd find yourself groping for your bread and trying to butter it like a blind person never taking your eyes off him lest his ego catch you taking five. But Willy Loman was suicidal. My dad doesn't have an iota of the depressive in him. He just depresses other people. Nothing brings him down. But this can't be true. I think it just comes out when absolutely no one else is around. It always seemed that while I knew he loved us a lot, my father actually needed nothing to be happy except books. There was enough in literature to challenge, entertain, amuse and inspire a man for a lifetime. Books and music were simply enough to sustain anyone was what he radiated. Humor, love, tragedy, it was all contained therein. And if all he needed was books, then he probably wouldn't mind if he lost the house and the wife and the whole life. Because the story was more important than the family. The story being that he was going to write the Great American Novel and finally be important, and in being important, he would be loved. Willing to lose his family to be loved by his family. Oh, the tragic blunder of this. It could almost drive someone mad. Wait, it did drive someone mad.

WHEN HE WASN'T IN his office, my dad hung around the kitchen, talking about Fitzgerald and reading aloud to my mother from a book of poetry by Keats, pointing out what Fitzgerald had stolen from Keats. I really think it was this kind of undergraduate behavior, lolling about reading poetry aloud and listening to *Don Giovanni* during lunch, that drove my mother into the arms of people like Barbara Taylor Brad-ford. She wanted to be left alone to flip through Jacques Pépin cookbooks and smoke and nap. My dad used to lament his predicament to me. "Jean-Joe, if I could do anything else I would. In a second." He was letting me know the deal with writing and by extension, my lunch money. And maybe his relationship with Mom, his marriage. You didn't write because you wanted to, you wrote because you had to. Mom was "livid, absolutely livid" six days out of seven. She had been supportive when they had four babies on a reporter's income, when he moved us all to New York to write a novel, when the job at CBS ended and he didn't get another one but started a second novel. She was running out of encourage-ment. I would worry about it at night, trying to fall asleep. "What the hell is going to happen to Dad?"

DUMBENTIA

Mom's summa cum laude routine got a little old after a few hundred mentions, and she'd never really had a job. Dad was a really good writer but he hadn't written the Great American Novel. The stories about who we were, who they were, didn't seem to match anything I saw. If we're such longtime Catholics, if our ancestors built cathedrals, why do we go to church only twice a year, bombed out of our minds? If writers are so goddamn fascinating, why do they monopolize conversations and talk about their "projects" until you're about ready to throw your sandwich at their heads? Dad's artistic struggle, our financial high-wire act, meant that we were, I was, building character. Whatever the fuck that was. Their marriage seemed blighted. But they expected a hell of a lot from us. My mother was a stay-in-bed mom and my father was a stay-at-home writer, so I couldn't help thinking, Why do I have to work so hard when you people sit around and drink coffee all day and pretend to do things?

———

These two layabouts demanded top performance in school, and socially we were supposed to be charming, entertaining, and "presentable." If I had it right, I was supposed to have the manners of Tracy Lord from *The Philadelphia Story* and the mind of Murray Kempton. You couldn't let your mouth hang open otherwise you'd look apish; a straight back was crucial, no gum chewing, but smoking cigs was well, there were worse things a teenager could do. Manners were everything, unless some investment banker at a cocktail party, some Solomon Brothers jackass, glanced at his watch as you talked about your novel outline, in which case it was okay to call him a horse's ass, and definitely not out of line to throw a drink in his face. Growing up, I thought throwing a drink in someone's face was the most natural thing in the world. You like someone? Ask him what you can get him to drink. Dislike someone? Throw a drink in his face. And yet our table manners—using the right fork, knowing the right way to cut meat, the right way to lean the fork at the top of the plate when you were finished—were constantly scrutinized. Now, if you wanted to stab someone in the temple with that fork during dinner, that was fine, just for heaven's sake know where to place the bloody fork on your plate when you were through.

WHAT MY FATHER PRESSED upon me even more than his family being an old St. Louis family was the fact that we were also, as far as he could trace our ancestral beginnings, not math people. I remember my mother reading aloud from the *New York Times* science section about right-brain/left-brain theories. She loved to identify with right brainers, to distance herself from "lefties" (engineers, lawyers, people who could add 7 plus 6 and come up with 13) as much as possible. It seemed to me growing up that my mother used the number forty-five so often ("I've asked you forty-five times to pick up your room," "That dog has pooped under the dining room table forty-five times this week") simply because it was one of the few numbers she knew. If there was one area of their marriage that was quite strong it was their mutual disapproval of math. They did the best they could to keep math out of our house and it may have been, for us, the subject non grata even more than God. They were more than happy to discuss and many times actually do my schoolwork for me if they found the subject matter lively enough. When I studied Greek and Roman history in Mr. Shaw's sixth-grade class my dad built me a Trojan horse and my mom had painstakingly fashioned a gorgeous clay Julius Caesar figurine with a knife sticking out of his chest and twenty-three plops of Heinz ketchup around his body on the steps of the Senate building indicating the twenty-three times Caesar was stabbed. My dad wrote plenty of papers for me. He showed real promise on a ten-pager about Saint Thomas Aquinas, but usually he got terrible grades at Bronxville High School, where his obscure and plentiful high literary references—from Chaucer's *Canterbury Tales* to a Voltaire pun to the thick of Faulkner—usually lost teachers. That, or they couldn't pass my father's lack of a decent five-paragraph funnel essay. But I was still expected to pass math class.

When summer school in algebra became a distinct possibility, my parents hired the Harvard-bound daughter of their only friends, the other Democrats in Bronxville, Bill and Suzanna Dean, to tutor me. Bill and Suzanna would come over and have drinks in the kitchen with my parents while April and I sat upstairs at my desk, directly above the kitchen, going over parabolas for the fiftieth time. I didn't understand a thing April said but I responded with phrases like "Isn't that interesting?" and "Ah! I see. I didn't get that before," as I was the host and didn't want my guest to feel awkward. In addition to April I also had my algebra teacher, Mrs. Peterson, tutoring me a couple times a week after school. I just didn't get the shit. When I came home after school one day and told them I had indeed failed algebra and would need to go to Scarsdale summer school, my mother asked me if I had been nice to Mrs. Peterson.

"You catch more bees with honey than you do with vinegar," my mother said as I cried on her bed. My mother had gone to Villa Duchesne, a Catholic school in St. Louis where the chaste young girls strolled the verdant campus wearing sweaters with "VD" emblazoned on the chest and where apparently a good shampoo would do just as well as a pencil in solving fractions. "Honestly, with that dirty hair the nuns wouldn't have passed me, either," she told me.

From her point of view, math was a social problem that

could be solved with a few well-placed compliments and clean hair. "We're not mathematicians, dolly. But you can pass a class. You just don't care."

I had timed it so I could tell my mom while Eleanor, Katharine and Julia were out. Failure had two parts: the part between you and your fuck-up and the part between your three sisters and your fuck-up. There would not be a scene of feminine compassion and empathy. (Don't worry, Jean. You'll make a good life for yourself somewhere where decent people can't add or subtract.) No, there'd be a lot of "What? You FAILED algebra?" and "What's wrong with you?" And then one of them would say, in John Merrick's voice, "I am not an id-i-ote!" Eleanor was no Rhodes scholar but she wasn't aiming to be, she was a theater person. Katharine was a very good student and cared about grades and getting into a good college, so she thought I was just a reckless individual. Academics weren't the passion of Julia's life—her two interests were "cruising" with her friends and cruising with her boyfriend J.J.—but she was a solid B student.

WITH THIS F, I was now officially on "double probation," which meant that I could not participate in any sports after school, which was fine by me. If I was too lazy to open a book, why in the world would I want to spend my afternoons running down a field in a hideous tartan skirt with a supersized boomerang in my hand, trying to hit a small ball into another girl's overdeveloped calves?

By junior year, although I showed absolutely no interest, I was being prepped for college and I found myself on interviews at schools I would never get into.

"What are three adjectives other people would use to describe you as a person?" the interviewer at the University of Vermont asked, looking up at me from a manila folder on the desk.

Three seems awfully limited as far as seventeen years of living goes—can we really be expected to have accumulated only three self-describing adjectives? What about faults and weaknesses? Everyone has those, so should I include those in the three? I'm smart, attractive and gassy? I'm clear-complected, a good eater, and violent when drunk? Also, which people describing us are we talking about? Are we talking about my parents? Because they might say I'm a naturally good speller, articulate and don't live up to my potential. Teachers, on the other hand, might say I'm foul-mouthed, lazy and unscrupulous. My sisters could very well opt for: ham-handed, moochy, and dragon-breathed. If the question was posed to my boyfriend, he'd probably lean toward flat-chested, thoughtless and pretty. My friends would go for daring! hilarious! and INSANE! Sit me in that admissions director's assistant's intern's office chair today and I might choose wrinkleless, goal-free and alcoholic in describing my teenage self.

My parents had contracted a bad case of Bronxville's ivy-league fever.

"I'll give Lattie Coor a call," my father said when I got home from my interview in Burlington. I told him I didn't really do so well and he came up with the idea of calling the president of UVM, Lattie Coor, someone he knew from St. Louis, to "call in a favor." My father always knows someone, someone who can get the job done, get you into that college; he knows editors of magazines, people who run theaters, and famous philanthropists, but not one deal has ever been closed on account of these connections, ever. These calls he makes are about as effective and insidery as chain letters. "We drove up together with a WU student to Wisconsin, La Crosse, to campaign for McCarthy—Lattie was provost at the time and trying to stay close to the kids. I'll give him a call after dinner."

I didn't mention to my dad that I had been totally hungover after doing blow and beer bongs all night at a frat party, that I'd been exhausted after employing my Jackie Chan maneuvers (my tendency to get all ass-kicky when drinking) to fight off trust-fund rapists, and could barely answer the questions I'd been asked at the interview. That stuff seemed like, well, a given.

I thought my problem was academic, Lazie-onnaire's disease, Layme Disease, Dumbentia. Because no one ever said anything about my drinking. We drank on weekends but also did a fair amount of drinking during actual school hours at Bronxville High School. We had daytime kegs at nearby Scout Field. When someone put a sock up on a post in the school courtyard in the morning that meant some people were going to the beer distributor in Tuckahoe to get a keg and there would be a party at "the field" around noon. "Sock's up" somebody would say, looking out the window of Mrs. Ribner's English class that overlooked the courtyard where the sock hung on a post. Apparently a beer smell coming off me in the middle of the day didn't seem unusual to teachers or my parents. Grades became everything but they had yet to weigh in on daytime drinking. When Katharine came home one night with twigs in her hair and said she had decided to take a little nap while walking home from a party and toppled into a pricker bush by the side of the road, it became one of the funny stories we told. The only rule we had around drinking was that Dad did not want us drinking before going out at night. Julia and I were having some beers before a party once and he came in and let us know that he didn't want us drinking before parties. No pre-drinking drinking.

Smoking wasn't particularly frowned upon, either. You couldn't smoke in front of Dad, from his own asthma he seemed to have some idea that children shouldn't smoke, but Mom didn't object too much as long as you didn't smoke her cigarettes. She kept her cartons of cigarettes in a drawer in the kitchen and she was beginning to notice that packs were being opened rather savagely as if by a novice. Julia and I denied smoking her brand and were vindicated when the novices turned out to be rats living in our basement who would come up into the kitchen drawers at night and eat her cigarettes. Her children smoking her stash was bad enough, but rats, they could damn well get their own cigarettes. She promptly called an exterminator.

My dad made me take Princeton Review, the SAT preparation course, on Saturday mornings. It was expensive, over five hundred dollars, and I went up ten whole points after taking it (not the kind of dramatic improvement they advertised). My father then decided I needed more one-on-one help, since that had worked such wonders with April Dean. He hired a tutor named Mr. Burnham to come on Sunday mornings. The first Sunday he came I forgot he was coming and had been out at some swanky party in the woods near the Metro-North train tracks with my friends. There was a knock on my bedroom door.

"Jean-Joe, are you decent? Mr. Burnham's here. Throw some sweatpants on and get downstairs. Posthaste."

I made my way downstairs and met Mr. Burnham. Unbeknownst to me, I had a giant hickey on my neck.

"Jesus, Jean-Joe, it looks like you were attacked by Cujo last night." My father put some spit on his finger and tried to rub the mysterious red blot with teeth marks off my neck.

"What in God's name is that?" my father said before I pushed him away and ran to the toaster to get a look.

The summer before my senior year in high school I got a break from SAT mania by going to Nantucket to be a mother's helper for my mother's friend from college. I had my driver's test coming up but I was supposed to be in Nantucket on the day of the test and I couldn't leave the job and come back and take my test for one day, so I came up with the logical solution of getting someone else to take it for me. If I had asked Eleanor or Katharine to take my road test, a felony, they would have thought of their futures, their ability to get jobs, have a clean record. Julia simply said, "Yeah, okay. What time?"

She did great. She passed. My dad was especially proud, mailing my new license to me with a short note, "Congratulations, Jean-Joe. You passed! Love, Dad."

Patty Henley had two boys, Christopher and Simon. They were five and eight. Mrs. Henley had just been left by her husband for a younger woman and she was fairly wrecked over it. Man, these class of '62 Manhattanville grads could cry at night. She had been spending summers in Nantucket for years, always renting the same house near her friends. This family had three gorgeous daughters, one of whom was an actress on a soap opera. That summer one of them was on crutches, and to me being a beautiful woman on crutches was an unbeatable combination. My sisters and I weren't allowed to break anything as we had no health insurance. I really envied anyone with a broken arm or leg. So extravagant! Maybe someday. I was friendless on that pink and green isle, so one night I decided to party by myself. Mrs. Henley was having dinner across the street at the Murphys', and Christopher and Simon were riding their bikes up and down the street. I went through the hall closet and found a big bottle of vodka, something I had never drunk before. I was a beer drinker, usually via funnel. I got drunk and wandered over to the Murphys' house and entered the living room, where people were sitting around enjoying a glass of wine, and in a blackout I started yelling, "Simon! Christopher! Get your bathing suits on! We're going to the beach!"

"Isn't that your mother's helper, Patty?" Mrs. Murphy said.

And then, according to what Mrs. Henley told me the next

morning, the two women carried me back to the house and put me to bed. The next day at breakfast when Mrs. Henley asked if I had been drinking, I said, "No, why?"

Dad could relate to my situation, I guess; in Bronxville he had no one to talk to, either—there were no artists around. (Local newscasters Bill Beutel and Chuck Scarborough lived there, hardly the Algonquin Round Table.) Mom was a phone person, but talking on the phone wasn't possible for me in Nantucket, there was always someone around. So writing letters became a way to tell my family about my job, my boss, a way to be miserable and have fun at the same time. Dad was the only person in the family who had time to write back, so we became pen pals. He was thrilled. My father thought I should compile all of my letters home and call them *Letters from a Mad Mother's Helper*. We signed off our letters with Andrews Sisters lyrics, "I sove you lo much, Dad" and "No bout a doubt it, Jean." It was probably the first time I saw language, formally put together as opposed to just whizzed around back and forth for comic effect, as a kind of fun. It was also the first time I saw that bad life equals good art. My miserable summer left me with a pile of funny letters home and a connection to what my father did or didn't do, a connection to him.

MY SENIOR YEAR in high school all my sisters were away at college. Things got particularly lonely when Julia went to college and I had to deal with Mom every night by myself. Mom's gloom was nocturnal; it came alive at night, after about seventeen glasses of Dewar's. When I'd pester her to perk up a little, easy on the drama, *s'il vous plaît*, she'd remind me, "I was born on Pearl Harbor, baby." Which wasn't true. She was born four days after Pearl Harbor, December 11, 1941, but if I brought up that fact she'd say, "Close enough, dearie." She fell off a horse at thirteen and broke her arm; she fell out her bedroom window at eleven and was in a leg cast for months; she drove her Thunderbird into a ravine, God damn it, she was legally blind; she was teeny, five feet, which isn't that much fun except when the Randy Newman song "Short People" came out, which she thought was "a riot." ("Oh, isn't that a riot?") But generally things were not a riot to my mother.

When I would call Katharine at Vassar, I'd tell her about the arguments on the front lawn, or the Sarah Lawrence professor my mother was convinced was Dad's lover, who mom was calling, screaming, every five minutes. I might as well have been living in a Blarney Stone bar near Grand Central, considering the tenor of the place. One Monday morning Mom had just disappeared.

"Mom's MIA. I think she took off to St. Croix to see Corky." Corky was a friend of my mom's from Villa Duchesne. "Are you reading?" I'd ask her.

"No," she'd snap back, long used to the accusation.

"It seems like you're reading," I said, from the pink Princess telephone in my room, which came from my grandmother's house in St. Louis. It still had her old exchange phone number

on the front, that Hitchcockian combination of words and letters. I loved it, not because I liked pink or irony, or was sen-
timental, but because the ringer was broken. I could call out
but was never disturbed by incoming calls in my bedroom.
The perfect form of communication in my mind, a model for
what I fantasized about in a romantic relationship.

"I'm listening. I'm listening! I heard you. Mom's MIA in
Taos. Where'd she get the money to go to Taos?"

"She probably hocked something of Nonnie's. St. Croix.
You see you're not listening!"

"Taos. St. Croix. What's the diff? She'll come back eventually. With four hideous white sweatshirts with toucans on
them or something and that'll be that. I wouldn't worry too
much about it." Sound of a page turning. A thick turn, maybe
a magazine.

She wanted to help me become, not cool because that she
couldn't help me with, but me. Only less of an asshole. Doesn't
mean she stopped reading while I poured my guts out to her,
but she was there for me in some profoundly distracted way.

Katharine was herself a pragmatic person but unlike Eleanor, she admired risk-takers, she liked ideas and literature
and writers, she believed in people. She loved whatever part
of them was lovable and ignored the rest of them. This was
nothing less than a magic trick to me. How can you ignore
such gigantic, in Mom's case, lapses in judgment, strength,
maternal instinct? How can you discard the self-obsession of
her ilk? She went to fancy schools and owned horses and had
sports cars given to her at sixteen, and we were supposed to

feel bad that that was all over and had been replaced by, let's face it, us. Her sister, our aunt Ruth, was living her life in California and she wasn't turning to dust every night at five o'clock. People moved on. Didn't they? From some bullshit idea of what they thought they had coming to them? Somewhere? Somewhere, I was sure, there were people who moved on, people who realized how good they fucking had it and didn't go over the same stupid crap every night.

Mom had taken to occasionally sleeping on an orange cot on the lawn and Katharine would come home for a weekend and simply pull up a chair and bring out some iced tea and the *New York Times* Sunday crossword, and the two of them would spend the day in the sun drinking iced tea and deliberating over a six-letter word for the opposite of a bad design (W-R-I-G-H-T).

I WAS FURIOUS AT MOM, and yet I also knew I was an alcoholic like her from the first time I drank. I guzzled tons of champagne at Eleanor's graduation party and before I went to bed I stole another bottle of it and put it in an old dirty tire that was in the way back of the Torino for my next drinking binge. I woke up and hardly remembered anything of the party. I remembered a champagne fountain and strawberries and drinking with Julia and then I remembered stealing the champagne. I dragged myself out of bed and ran to the car to make sure it was still there. I knew this was a little odd. To wake up in the morning and locate my next drink. I knew it wasn't normal to not remember things when drinking. I knew I was like Mom. This was not good. So how, I thought, how can I get away with it? How can I drink and not turn into Mom? I guess don't get married, don't own a chaise longue, don't smoke (too late), don't be five feet tall, okay good, I'm already five feet five, don't be rich and spoiled, check, don't cry all the time, no problem, don't dye your hair blond, okay. Most of all don't drink Dewar's scotch. Now, that's easy. Maybe I could do this.

THE TREASURER'S
REPORT

To KNOW MY FATHER is to know "The Treasurer's Report," a monologue written by Robert Benchley of the Algonquin Round Table. It was written in 1922 for a live revue show and later made into a short film starring Benchley. I don't remember a time when he wasn't pushing it on us. Benchley plays an assistant treasurer for a boys' club who is forced to go on for the absent treasurer at the annual dinner gala and give the financial report of the organization. He's the world's biggest bumbler but in a very endearing way, giving this dry, dry report. It is a very funny piece but as outdated as my dad's wooden shoehorns. It felt like old white guy stuff to us. He had gotten us to love old white guy stuff like the Andrews Sisters and Abbott and Costello and the Marx Brothers, but these could pass for entertainment, whereas the Benchley piece was literature, albeit comic, found in a book (we hadn't seen the short film) on our living room bookshelves called *The Treasurer's Report and Other Aspects of Community Singing*. It was just the kind of writing that Dad would bring up over and over again for us to "try."

As a kid I was absolutely terrified of clichés. My father forbade them in our home. It was like the way other people regarded cursing in their house. If you said, "You can lead a horse to water, but you can't make him drink," my father would go ballistic. Mom couldn't control herself, apparently, because she violated this rule about every five seconds.

I was under the impression clichés could ruin you, ruin your life, your hopes and dreams, bring down your whole operation if you didn't watch it. They were gateway language, leading straight to a business major, a golfy marriage, needlepoint pillows that said things about your golf game, and a self-inflicted gunshot to the head that your family called a heart attack in your alma mater announcements. Character suicide. Language was important, sexy, fun, alive, extremely personal, it was like food, you wouldn't just pop anything into your mouth, why would you let anything pop out that hadn't been considered and prepared for someone to enjoy? To ignore language was akin to ignoring the very person you were speaking to, rude, uncaring, unfeeling, cold. It was a way to connect and also to woo, to charm, to manipulate, it was a tool for love, for survival. Your words were you. To ignore language was to ignore Dad. To love words was to love Dad.

MY FATHER HAD EXTREMELY strong feelings about what was okay to read and what was not. I was completely intimidated by his literary standards and expectations and to this day it seems amazing and daring to me that other people will just read something without thinking much about it. "Oh, I found that book in my living room. I don't know where it came from. My babysitter must have left it here." Your baby-sitter? You just read whatever's lying around? Are you crazy? You think you're gonna make it to fifty living like that? My father asked in every conversation, "So what are you reading these days?" I always knew it was coming, I agonized over whether to lie or not.

He was like the Great Santini of the Strand. Few people could take him on; he was so well-read and had a memory that could retain every detail of everything he'd ever read, as well as jokes, lyrics, arias, names of store owners he'd met on his honeymoon in Paris, names of restaurants where gang-sters were gunned down in 1924. He could quote lines from books he disliked better than you could quote lines from what you claimed was your favorite book of all time. The list of acceptable writers to bring up included: T. S. Eliot, Faulkner, Woody Allen's humor pieces (and movies), Robert Benchley, Dorothy Parker, Zelda Fitzgerald, F. Scott Fitzgerald, Keats, James Joyce, Yeats, Wordsworth, Marcel Proust, Joseph Conrad, H. L. Mencken, Norman Mailer, Murray Kempton, Edmund Wilson, Ring Lardner, Henry James, Shakespeare, Evelyn Waugh (I remember repeating "E-vlyn, E-vlyn" to myself around the house when I was about fourteen, terrified I'd slip and pronounce it like an American woman's name), D. H. Lawrence, Dos Passos, Nabokov, Chekhov, Twain and Hemingway, and composers like Leonard Bernstein, Mozart,

Cole Porter and Fats Waller. Contemporary writing was only for people who might live forever, otherwise, the point was the greats.

He was always letting you know, huh, huh, who was in charge. You think you can sit around reading what we read when we read Raymond Carver all summer? You've got another thing coming, baby. He wouldn't let you spend too much time talking about popular writers. If I was really pissed at him I might mention this "amazing!" John Fante novel I was halfway through. If I was getting a kick out of the plays of Christopher Durang, he'd say, "Oh, well, if you're getting serious about farce, you can't beat Oscar Wilde. What about the French? Have you tried Feydeau?" Like most people I thought e. e. cummings was delightful, a poet so playful he attracts teenagers and college students, but e. e. cummings was too bloody easy: easy easy cummings, Frank O'Hara? Too easy. There was always someone better, harder to read that he would divert your attention to: Keats or Shelley, for example.

"Jean-Joe, have you given that Ring Lardner I gave you a try yet?" Lardner's book *Haircut* is a favorite of my father's.

"My God, is that funny. Not a false note in it. Give it a try."

The writers you were strongly discouraged from wasting your time on: Toni Morrison, anyone in the category of magical realism including Gabriel García Márquez and fantastic realism, Italo Calvino, historical fiction, Don DeLillo ("*White Noise* was absolute crap . . ."), Capote. Obviously anything inspirational was completely unacceptable, mass market anything, showing up to meet him for lunch with a John Grisham book under your arm would have been like showing up with no pants on, you know, get yourself together, for God's sake. Not even discussed, it would be so ludicrous.

If I could have calmed down a little I might have been a reader, but I was not a great, devoted or thorough reader. I loved family drama like Tennessee Williams, Arthur Miller, adored comic greats like Molière, Wilde, the essays of Woody Allen. I always wanted to be well-read, but I wasn't anywhere near well-read. Decently read, fantastically fakably read, motherfucking-lying-my-ass-off-to-your-face read. But it seemed like there was something more fun than books, like actual fun.

MY DAD HAD SPENT many years writing at five in the morning before he would go to work as a reporter at the *St. Louis Globe-Democrat*, years when he had four babies under five years old, a mailman-mauling dog named Wordsworth, and our pony, Pepsi, in the backyard, whose manure he would shovel before heading out to work. But now he wasn't getting up at five a.m. to write and he wasn't heading off to a job. He seemed to be losing something essential to being a writer. Or already had. Maybe it was getting older. Maybe it was Mom's drinking, which wasn't what you'd call ladylike, maybe it was his own drinking, maybe he lost his confidence after his second novel didn't sell. Dad wasn't writing anymore. Not that anyone talked about this while it was daylight outside. Now that he wasn't writing, it seemed like he talked about writing and books constantly, as if the fantasy was growing, had to grow if the reality was shrinking.

The first sign that he was no longer writing was he never mentioned submitting anything anymore, and then he wasn't talking at dinner about things he was writing, and then he wasn't even talking about things he was researching. He began talking about things he was *going to write* and this is pretty much where things stayed. Things he was going to write. At some future point. Until then, ideas went into tape recorders and file cabinets, all very carefully labeled, documented and organized.

I remember when we watched *The Shining*. The Torrances moved to that inn in Colorado so that Jack could work on his book, and then reality set in—the isolation—and the father went nuts. My mom groaned like a sick animal from the divan at the scene when Shelley Duvall sneaks into his writing room and peeks at his novel and sees that he has been typing "All work and no play makes Jack a dull boy" for months.

"Girls, turn it off. I can't watch. I simply can't watch," Mom said.

Dad's next project after his second novel, *Black Ink*, didn't happen was Stylebook, a computer program built to run on your writing, to improve your writing grammatically and stylistically. It was a genius idea. In 1984. When he began it. But it was starting to drag on with no end in sight. My dad hired some high schooler in New Jersey to build the software for Stylebook, and this kid, whom he called "the kid," ended up making tens of thousands of dollars working for my dad. He went off to college with every dime my dad scraped together and the program never ran properly. Some company offered my dad $300,000 for his research, but he felt this was peanuts compared with what it was going to do on the open market, so he declined this offer. Stylebook was an earnest attempt to make money and get Mom off his back and get back to writing. I was told this is the kiss of death, doing something in order to "get back to the writing." When you start doing this you're fucked, you have to stay on the writing always and do whatever you need to concurrently. I was told, "Never do anything in order to write. Don't take a job, don't even take a shower in order to write. You'll never get to the writing. You write." Dad was the person who told me this.

Stylebook was starting to drive Mom crazy. I knew he was going to get it handed to him. I saw him as a tragic hero. Like all tragic characters, he was trying to do the impossible—write novels, sell novels, make money, keep the drinking under control, get the cracked wife some help, take care of four kids. Like all tragic heroes he had a fundamental lack of self-awareness. Tragic characters don't go to therapy, read self-help, do juice fasts or see psychics. They go blind, they're banished from the kingdom, they hear ghosts. But they are good, noble in their pursuits, they just make bad decisions, have errors in judgment. He became increasingly saddening, if that's a correct term. Some people are maddening, Dad was saddening. If Mom kicked him out would he be able to avoid the kind of solitary, elderly poverty that Grandma Darst, Crazy Kate, wound up in?

LES MISSOURABLES

M Y FATHER MOVED his whole Stylebook operation into the kitchen. The kitchen was my mother's office, so they were now sort of working at the same company.

"The man has moved his goddamn word processor into the kitchen. MY kitchen! I'm about ready to have a breakdown here. I mean it."

Things were not good. Eleanor and Kate had to come home from college for a semester to work because Mom and Dad couldn't pay their tuition. Like a professional chef, Mom was never hungry by the time dinner came around, never really ate a meal with us. She took one bite, lit a cigarette and began a sort of post-shift meltdown. We were, of course, the customers she was complaining about.

"Nobody cares. Nobody cares," she would lament from her seat at the end of the dining room table as if she were all alone. "Do they have any idea how long it takes to fold those layers of white cake into the round *buche* shape without them falling apart in your hands? Hours. Hours! Do you think the

Smiths across the street are having homemade *bûche de Noël* tonight for dessert? Hardly."

We weren't ungrateful, we were simply too busy stuffing our faces with food to compliment her cooking. By the time dinner rolled around it was usually going on ten o'clock. We'd already had about two bowls of cereal each just to last until dinner.

"Well, I guess everyone hates the boeuf bourguignon," she'd sigh, brushing at a holey area of her shirt sleeve that had caught on fire earlier. When she said things like this I always imagined my father's old surf-casting fishing rod being cast in our direction.

"No, Mom, it's fantastic."

"Mmm, yeah, so good," Katharine would say.

"Doris, you've outdone yourself," my dad would chime in.

"No it's not. It's dry. It's dry and I'm going to bed." And she'd pick up her glass of wine and her cigarettes and she'd weave up the front staircase to her bedroom and shut the door. That was more or less how my mother now said good night.

One night I went into my parents' room and found my mother very upset and drunk.

"I'm going to do it. I am. I'm going to do it." My mother expressed a desire to die around this time every night. I hung my head. Every day was hard for her now.

"I'm going to jump," she said.

I looked at her and her body, slumped off to one side of the divan. She was approximately seven inches off the ground.

"Okay, well, whatever you think is best, Mom."

"I mean it, dolly. I'm going to jump."

"I understand." And I walked out of her bedroom.

Dad would never, ever utter the "a" word or even talk about it as even in the bag of things that might be wrong with Mom.

When I said to him a few days later, "I think Mom's an alcoholic," he said, "Your mother's not an alcoholic, she just thinks every night is New Year's Eve."

Maybe she had to drink so much because all that crying was drying her system out and making her thirsty. The crying was like a Tony Kushner play—it started one night and ended three nights later. "I'm dying! I'm dying, baby!" she'd call out as you were heading out the front door. "Daddy was never around, you know. Never a-round!" There was so much boohooing and theatrics that we did become fairly used to it. "I'm completely alone. ALONE! Did you hear what I said?" she'd wail as Julia and Katharine and I tried to watch a movie. "Yes, we heard you. We heard you. You're alone. Can you go be alone by yourself somewhere? We can't hear the movie."

Mom apparently decided to dust herself off and not be so alone, because she now had a friend in Bronxville. This was when things really got out of control. Kitty Lagasse was a drunk and a dress designer whose clothing line was kaput for unknown reasons. Kitty's husband, a Belgian toy maker, had died of an early heart attack, and so Kitty now supported herself making graduation and prom and cotillion dresses for Bronxville's junior set out of her house. Her work was inspired. She really did encourage bravery in her clients, her dresses asked you to be something more than you were, and you felt special when she yelled at you in the big, open living room of her small, modern house with the giant sloped glass window. "Stop schlumping your shoulders! For God's sake! You're becoming a woman, this is a good thing, throw away those old corduroys, let's move on! You're gonna be Ava Gardner just for one night if it kills me! Oh, these girls!" Kitty was the physical opposite of my mother; she was brunette and had a figure like Orson Welles. Kitty and my mother tended to get in a fair bit of trouble. They were like Lucy and Ethel, only completely besotted, coming up with ways to make money. Most of these ideas were never executed but one that did make it out of the barroom was their wine bags. They made beautiful gift bags for wine bottles with leftover fabric from Kitty's dresses (plaid taffeta and hot pink ribbons at the top). They were really nice and a good idea—there was nothing like them, but the bags never went anywhere.

Kitty had lavish tastes, which got out of control and led her to do things like occasionally stuff a ham in her coat at the A&P. There was always an international cast of characters at her house who seemed to be shooting a Fellini film in her backyard. There was a nineteen-year-old Belgian boy living in her basement whom she was apparently screwing, and another nefarious character who claimed he'd been hanging out with Joan Didion in Guatemala the week before and who, it turned out, had been looting temples in Guatemala, without Joan Didion, and was storing the artifacts in Kitty's basement.

Dad was not happy about this twosome at all. "That Kitty's got the scruples of an Arab slave dealer." Mom was no longer concerned with what Dad thought about anything. Or what any of us thought about what she was doing.

Her drinking was also completely out of control, which was infuriating, as I was trying to enjoy some out-of-control drinking myself. She was crowding the outfield.

One night I was at a kegger and my boyfriend walked up to me with a queer look on his face.

"Your mom's here."

Even though I was semi-smashed I understood the implications of one's mother showing up at a kegger. I looked around at the groups of kids, my eyes scanning the CB ski jackets quickly, running over the Bronxville High School football jerseys, desperately trying to locate the small woman hell-bent on squashing my existence.

I hated Petey at this moment. I hated his jokey stockbroker father and his super-nice paddle-tennis-playing nonsexual yet attractive mother-woman, Pepper. I hated him for having an expensive car and for the fact that he didn't black out and forget portions of evenings.

"She's over there, pumping the keg, talking to Dennis McSweeney."

"Great. Fucking great."

"Doesn't look like she's here to break up the party."

At that point I saw Dennis McSweeney stick his finger into my mother's beer, showing her how to make the foam go down. My mother laughed and stuck her finger in her own beer as well. I walked over.

"Jean!" my mother yelped.

"Your mom's the kegmeister now, Darst," Dennis said.

"Is Petey here?" my mom said, but before I could get my mitts on her, I heard Kitty's crazy drunkard voice coming toward us. She slurred her speech drunk or sober, but Kitty also had a broken volume-control button so her voice often just flew randomly into a much louder volume.

"Doris? Doris, where the hell are you? I'm LOST IN A SEA of tedious rugby shirts, oh God, NOTHING BUT PRIMARY COLORS, it's really unbearable. Doris?" Kitty made it to the keg.

My mother pumped the keg and filled Stu Patterson's red plastic cup with foamy beer. "How about a brewski?" Stu laughed and stuck his finger in his beer. "You might want to tilt the cup a little when you fill it, Mrs. Darst, keeps the foam down."

"Okay, dear. Will do."

"Mom, let's go home. C'mon." We locked eyes. Hers seemed to say, "Why would I want to leave this terrific party to go home with boring old you?"

"Doris, I have to agree," Kitty said. "YOU'RE DOING a great job with that keg, but I'm JUST NOT A BEER PERSON. God, they don't even have any wine at this party. Oh, these kids, I can't stand it. The money, all the money these parents are shelling out for this ridiculous PRISON WEAR. What's wrong with a great Geoffrey Beene wool suit? Or how about a FABULOUS FITTED JACQUARD BLAZER WITH A PAIR OF JEANS? I'm leaving, Doris."

Kitty went home and I managed to wrest Mom away from her duties as kegmeister and walk her down the street back to our house. When we got there, I found Eleanor and Kate on the glass porch watching *Saturday Night Live*.

"Guess where I've been?"

They were hoping I might wait for a commercial to bug them. "Where?"

"At the Landers', down the street."

"Oh."

"Yeah, they had a party. Guess who was there?"

"I don't know. Who?"

"Mom. Mom was at the party."

Eleanor and Kate started giggling. Kate put a needlepoint pillow of a Picasso figure up to her face to hide her laughing.

Eleanor wanted to make sure she didn't miss any more *Saturday Night Live*, so she jumped in: "Look, Jeanne, Mom said she was going to this party down the street. What were we supposed to do?"

"I tried to stop her, Jeanne," Kate said, laughing even harder. "I swear."

"Jeanne, you know you can't stop Mom when she's going to do something," Eleanor said, picking up the clicker, preparing to unmute the TV.

"Right. Because she's five-feet-zero and there are two of you guys."

"Maybe no one noticed her at the party. She's so teeny, no one probably even saw her except you," Kate said, drying her eyes with her T-shirt.

"Yeah, no one noticed a forty-three-year-old in a black pencil skirt and panty hose doing beer bongs with Hugh Masterson."

Kate gasped. Hugh Masterson was the first guy she'd made out with. "No!"

"And Kitty knocked over about five people on the way out."

"Okay, shush, it's Father Guido Sarducci," Eleanor commanded.

IT GOT QUIET around the house. Mom and Dad stopped going at each other—verbally, nonverbally, Mom throwing wine bottles at Dad, charging at him, slipping once and getting a black eye—and started going away from each other. Attacking each other we understood, moving away was more complicated. A war was upon Eleven Hamilton Avenue. My mother's base of operations was my parents' bedroom, while my father had set up camp in Eleanor's presidential suite on the third floor once Eleanor and Katharine went back to school. My mother wanted everyone's sympathy. Dad wanted her to straighten up and be the old mama, the mama who was game for anything, the mama who thought he was wonderful, exciting, brilliant and talented. Or in her terms, "the cat's meow."

That kind of time travel was not on her agenda. Instead, Mom came out as a Republican. She had worked on Dad's campaign for president of the board of aldermen in St. Louis, so this was hurtful to him and went against everything his family had done for the poor and for civil rights.

With everyone else at college Mom and Dad waited for me to graduate from high school so they could sell the house and get divorced. I felt like I was a slow eater and the check had been paid and everyone had their coats on still sitting at the table, waiting for me to be finished.

Meanwhile, Mom planned.

AS SOON AS I graduated she would move into the city where she belonged. She was a city person, in case we didn't realize this about her. She was unable to get by one more minute without Korean delis and takeout and gay colorists for confidantes. We didn't know. Dad, during the in-house separation, was vulnerable, emotionally but also, obviously, financially. And I felt awful for him.

Mom stopped cooking for Dad. She would make dinner and then as we were eating, Dad would come in the kitchen and chat cheerfully as he always did, only he would be preparing some really disgusting dinner for himself. Olives and some chicken livers. This was what he could afford. We were eating salad, leg of lamb, while Dad was sautéing chicken livers and a hunk of bread. He ate chicken livers four out of five nights. It seemed to me the most depressing thing in the world that someone should be banished from the family meal, made to eat something different, something inferior. Dad was helpless in the kitchen. He had no money, no cooking skills, no ideas about what to eat, really. There was no staff in the kitchen to prepare him a plate where he could sit and talk about working for the white man. He was fending for himself for probably the first time in his life. And I would rather not have watched.

My mother seemed like Idi Amin eating her lamb in front of my father. Had she not studied the Geneva Convention? They were at war, yes, but there were rules. Food is life, theoretically, so if you stop cooking for someone, are you trying to kill them? It seemed to me this is precisely what she was trying to do.

ONE MORNING DAD ASKED me how to use the washing machine and I didn't know so we tried to figure it out together when Mom came in and said she was putting the house on the market.

She had a prescient relationship with real estate well before people made livings as house flippers or devoured TV shows about making a killing selling a house. She just had a sense, which she had worked a few times in St. Louis before we moved to New York. She was like Columbo, being driven around in some real estate agent's Cadillac.

"You want to buy the worst house on the best street," she'd say, chopping cucumbers in the kitchen. She prided herself on the fact that she had found our house, a house that was in her mind a piece of crap but one that was way up in value. When she sold it she really got into the fact that she had made so much money on it, like she had hoodwinked some suckers into paying through the nose for an illusion, for her illusion, one that she had birthed and paid for with her own money, suffered for, and was now unloading. She was "staging" before there was a word for it. I came home one day with my boyfriend, Martin, to find her tinkering with her mise-en-scène.

"Martin, Jeanne. I need you to sit in the living room."

"But we were going to watch *The Edge of Night* upstairs in Julia's room."

"Well, I need you to put a decent shirt on and grab a book, Dickens or better yet, *Jane Eyre*, and sit in front of the fire on the living room floor."

"Fire? It's seventy-two outside."

"Do as I say!" she snapped, and then went into the kitchen to put a gizmo in the oven that emits the smell of baking apple pie throughout your house.

We changed our shirts quickly and got in front of the fire and pretended to be reading on the carpet while strangers came through our house and looked into closets and asked about property taxes. She sold our house for five times what she bought it for, in just under four hours.

My graduation, the thing that my parents were waiting for, was almost upon us, but the spring before I was supposed to go to college I had nowhere to go. I had gotten into George Washington University and Boston University but was partying too much to read my acceptance letters, which asked for deposits to secure a space. So I had nowhere to go. My mother and I drove to Washington, D.C., to convince George Washington University to let me in even though their fall class was now full. My mother's version of "making a few phone calls" was to put in a physical appearance, as if she were a celebrity whose name the admissions committee failed to see on my application. "Perhaps you didn't recognize the name? Doris Gissy Darst, child equestrian? Cover of *Sports Illustrated*, 1956? Youngest person ever on the cover until Nadia Comăneci?" Surely there had to be someone my mother could take out for a drink that would "get it" about my situation. Apparently there was not. We drove home. A few weekends later, in late May, my mother took Eleanor with her to the State University of New York at Purchase, having Eleanor fill out an application form for me in the car on the way there. I must have been accepted because my parents dropped me and a few suitcases off there for Orientation Weekend in late August. I didn't go shopping with my mom for new bedspreads and shower caddies and framed posters of Degas ballet dancers. As mother and daughter we made no lists of things I would need, picked out no special sweaters for the fall classes, we didn't figure out how I would call home or when I would check in with her. My mother told me to watch out for the food, that it would have a lot of starch in it that would make me gain weight. That was about it for preparations and going-off-to-college bonding. I brought my old bedspread and my pillows and some towels from the bathroom and I got in the car. I was set up with a meal plan and given some money and then they gave me a hug and took off. College. No big deal. Just like I suspected.

CRABS AND REHABS

MY BOYFRIEND, Martin, pointed to the light on his desk, the twisty neck of which was pulled down, like a microscope, over a sheet of loose-leaf paper.

"Look," he said.

Martin was twenty-four to my eighteen; we had begun dating in my junior year in high school and then he had followed me to college, although we never talked about this—one day he just said he was going to college also, my college. It wasn't hard to get in, you could pretty much call the morning you wanted to come and start that day. So he did. And it wasn't going well. I'm the youngest kid—I don't like anyone following me.

"Get under the light. Really get in there," he insisted.

I bent over the desk and looked at the light's circle.

"What is that, a pube?"

"Yes, mine. What else do you see, Jeanne?"

I leaned in again, wondering why Martin had to act so bananas all the time. And then I saw it. A teeny little black creature on the pube.

"Is that a flea?"

"I wish it were, Jeanne."

"Well, what is it then, Martin?"

"You don't know what it is? You have no idea?"

"No."

"It's a crab, Jeanne."

"A crab?"

"Yes, a crab. A louse. A pubic louse?" Martin yelled. His room-mate, Mark, a Keene State transfer student who was a "nontra-ditional" student (read: older, loser), like Martin, walked in.

Martin glared at me, which was confusing. If he found lice in his mattress, shouldn't he let Mark know their room had bugs?

"Let's go," Martin said, swiping the loose-leaf sheet of paper off the desk and dropping it in the garbage. Mark hung his coat up in the closet.

"Later, man," Martin said.

"Later," Mark said.

I was about to say, "Later," but it seemed like it would have been too many.

Martin walked quickly ahead of me. When we got a little way down the hall he turned back and yelled, "You fucked somebody over Thanksgiving break. I can't believe you fucked somebody!" A drowsy, bathrobed student walked past us to the hall bathroom with her little pink plastic bathroom caddie.

"I did not fuck anybody over Thanksgiving." I had drunk-enly made out with a couple people but they'd have to have a pretty bad case of crabs to transmit them to me that way. "This is what I'm talking about, Martin. These wacko accusations."

"Well, then where the fuck did I get crabs? Huh?"

"Would you relax? Maybe you got them from the sweatpants I stole from the gym."

The New York Knicks had taken over the school's gym, the least used gym ever constructed on American soil, SUNY Purchase being an arts school. Other than the couple hours a week that the acting department practiced fencing there it was totally deserted. So the New York Knicks took it over and now the parking lot was full of BMWs and Cadillacs and seven-foot-tall men roamed the halls of the gym, asking me if I'd seen their massage therapist. Their lackey would come by "the cage" and dump their gargantuan sweats in the laundry machines behind my desk. The cage was the name of the check-in area where I worked, which housed fencing swords and face nets and squash rackets. I checked IDs and handed out towels to sweaty actors who wrapped them around their necks like Kate Hepburn walking the Connecticut shore in 1942. Mostly I sat at the desk and read because hardly anyone ever came through.

One day I stuffed some of the Knicks sweatpants into my backpack. It wasn't like their financial officer was going to shut down the franchise because of a bloated sweatpants budget. When I got them back to my dorm I realized I'm five-seven. These sweats, while seriously thick and plush and a nice classic navy color, were about a foot too long. You couldn't roll them up, either, because the cuff was so thick your ankles looked like you had elephantiasis. I cut them and made shorts out of them.

The other problem with the stolen sweats was that they didn't say "New York Knicks" on them anywhere, so I'd trot them out expecting enormous recognition for my winning shorts but to other people they just looked like navy cutoff sweatpant shorts.

"Aren't these shorts cool?" I'd say to Emma, my friend from the city.

"They all right. They're not all that if that's what you're askin'."

"They're New York Knicks sweats."

Emma looked me up and down. "They don't say New York Knicks."

"That's because these are their private sweats. You know, like their private collection. These are theirs, not that mass-marketed shit for fans. You can't buy these."

"So where'd you get 'em?"

"I stole them."

"Oh."

"Yeah. From the gym. From the Knicks."

"Oh. That's cool."

"Yeah, that's what I'm saying. They wear these. They rehearse in these."

"Practice. The Knicks don't rehearse. Shit."

So I had to have this long, tiring conversation before I'd get the recognition I deserved. It just wasn't worth the trouble.

At an arts school, no one's impressed with the Knicks. If they had been sweats that Kevin Kline rehearsed in while doing Shakespeare in the Park with Meryl Streep, somebody might have given a fuck.

"I don't think I got crabs from Patrick Ewing," Martin said. "I only wore those once and then I waxed my car with them. They were too goddamn big."

By the time I deduced that I got the crabs from borrowing a nightgown over Thanksgiving break from one of my best friends from high school, Maggie, a real traditional Westchester slut, I was no longer concerned with proving my fidelity to Martin. Martin had become a man who commented on my "freshman fifteen" and forced me to go jogging around campus with him, a man who knew I had become bored by him, a man who was obsessed with Tiffany's. More than any young marriage-crazed woman from New Jersey, that man loved that little robin's-egg-blue box. He was always giving me necklaces and bracelets from there. He even gave my three sisters Elsa Peretti necklaces at Christmas. Martin could be too traditional. Like when I peed in my bed when he slept over one night after a big night of drinking he acted like an outraged English butler he was so crispy about it. My feeling was I'm sorry if my urinating in the bed, my bed by the way not your bed, interferes with some kind of image you have of me, but just because you give me things from Tiffany's doesn't mean I'm the girl in the Tiffany's ad in the *New York Times Magazine* and/or it doesn't mean the girl in the Tiffany's ad doesn't pee in the bed when she drinks too much. Why don'cha put a lid on it and help me flip this mattress over so we can go back to getting a little shut-eye?

After three days of lathering each other up angrily with anti-louse shampoo we got from the campus nurse, I broke it off with Martin and was catching a train into the city for Christmas break. As I waited for my cab to the White Plains train station, he said, "I just don't think this is over," meaning us. I said I was pretty sure it was and tossed my little plastic lice comb into the garbage, and scratched my crotch one last time.

"Merry Christmas, Martin."

I woke up one morning about three days into Christmas break and got up and made coffee. Julia continued to snooze on the pull-out we were sharing. If there was one person you didn't want on your pull-out it was Julia; she might not ever get up and she needed only a few short hours to transform any room into a Hooverville.

I sat at a table near the pull-out with my coffee, absent-mindedly itching my cooch, wondering how she passed anything at school. "Jules, are you ever getting up?"

She rolled over and looked at me. "Is something up your heinie?"

"No. I just thought we should get up. It's eleven-thirty. Mom hates to come out and have there be pillows and bedding everywhere at noon."

"Well, then she shouldn't have gotten a one-bedroom."

Julia stayed at Mom's on breaks even though she had a dorm room on University Place.

She rolled away from me and pulled the covers over her head. Getting up for another cup of coffee, I saw Julia's hand come up out of the covers and rake her curly blond head a few times hard. Then she got off the pull-out and started toward the bathroom, all the way scratching at her crotch. In the kitchen I put my cup on the counter and froze. I realized that not only did I still have the dreaded pubic vermin but now my sister might have them as well. I scratched my crotch and tried to think. I heard the clinking sound of the chain on my mother's bedside lamp hitting the porcelain base. She'd be lighting a cigarette momentarily and groping for her glasses. Mom, now that she lived alone, could indulge her most Plathian tendencies. Rather than waking up and opening the blinds in her bedroom, she now woke up and turned on lights. It seemed like the most hopeless thing to me. Day was something to get through, a stepping-stone to night, to drunkenness, sleep, and when she had had enough, death.

MY MOTHER HAD TIMED leaving my father so I could almost hear the curtain coming down on their marriage as I walked off the stage of the Bronxville High School auditorium with my temporary dummy diploma. When she moved from Bronxville into Manhattan after the divorce, she rented a two-bedroom for five women, which seemed rather short-sighted. We had just come from a five-bedroom house, so we knew something was up. Then Mom moved to a one-bedroom and shortsighted met statement.

The place was on Eighty-seventh Street, a half a block from the mayor's mansion in Yorkville. It was called Garson Towers. Residential buildings with names, unless you were talking about the Ansonia or the Apthorp or somewhere swanky, were depressing to me. They seemed like the kinds of places lonely, defenseless elderly people got murdered. My mother's maiden name was Gissy, and seeing that she seemed to be preparing to audition for any number of Tennessee Williams plays, retelling stories of her privileged youth over and over, we began calling the building "Gissy Towers." If you were going to spend some people's entire childhoods getting tanked on Dewar's talking about your coming-out party at the Fleur-de-Lis Ball and crying about how Daddy never said he loved you, well, you were in for some shit, in our opinion. But in fact a Williams character like Blanche DuBois was a sharp-eyed futurist, a trailblazing entrepreneur, she was Buckminster Fuller; Blanche DuBois was Steve Jobs compared to my mother.

Mom's bedroom door opened and the smell of smoke wafted into the living room, preceding her like applause for an old theater broad's entrance.

She entered the kitchen in some ridiculous silken Natori number, a robe that screamed, "I'm sleeping with my divorce lawyer," to conjure up a cup of coffee for herself. I straightened myself to make my thoughts disappear, to make my crab-addled mind impossible to read.

"Morning," I said. "I made coffee."

"Morning, dolly. Did you use the Illy?" she said, passing me with her cigarette. My mother was like a bat with her lit cigarettes. She came impossibly close to you, you were convinced you were going to have to drop and roll any second, but somehow she always just missed you. I resisted the impulse to say anything about her cigarette, as we lived in a world, since selling our house, that was no longer ours but hers.

"Yeah, I did. It's delish."

"It's Italian."

Mom glided over and sat at the table. "Where's Julia?"

"In the bathroom," I said, sipping guiltily.

"What are you girls up to today?"

"Christmas shopping I guess."

"I'm going out with Mr. Sully tonight so you girls will have to get some dinner for yourselves." Her divorce lawyer who was taking her for a huge ride, the kind of ride where someone leads you to believe they will leave their wife for you when the time is right, was Mr. Sully. "I'll leave you some money. You can get a pizza or go to Melon's and get a burger if you want."

Julia came out of the bathroom.

"Good morning, Julia," Mom said. With her deep voice she might have been Lauren Bacall greeting Bogie after a wild night.

"Hunfh shew naggeh," Julia mumbled, and kept going.

"Honestly," Mom said, widening her eyes.

Chitchat had never been Julia's bag.

Doris was forty-four. This was when forty-four was forty-four, before it was the new thirty-four and sixty-four was the new fifty-four and eighty-four was the new seventy-four and twenty-four was the new fourteen, but even so, she looked fantastic, had some dough in the bank after selling the house, and she might have gone off and done all kinds of things: opened a bike shop in Costa Rica, started an adoption agency for American gay men in places where communism has fallen, waited tables in a pub in Britain's seaside town of Cornwall. But this was back when forty-four was the age when women aged, fell apart—although according to my father, the "decline," as he called it, actually started when she was a straight-A student at Manhattanville College embarking on her maiden breakdown, an event that was interrupted when she married and had four kids.

My mother's rehab years began when her four daughters went off to college. It was as if rehabs were her way of going back to college with all of us kids, eating bad food and being homesick. This seemed like a misguided attempt at youth, getting out of the house, enriching the mind. Had my mother not heard of postgraduate work?

I had gone to the pharmacy the day I got in from Purchase, and charged a couple bottles of RID to Mom's account, but the apartment was so small there never seemed to be a good time to exterminate myself. My plan was to chemical myself silly at night when everybody had gone to bed. Problem was, I kept falling asleep before Mom and Julia. To stay up past Julia one really had to have street drugs of some kind.

I began monitoring Julia for signs of crab life. I told myself the initial itching I witnessed during my first seven cups of coffee might have been nothing more than the traditional crotch-scratching one does as a guest in another's home while people are having breakfast. I was disabused of this notion when I caught sight of Julia scratching herself in the elevator and then later while we were Christmas shopping at Orva on Eighty-sixth Street. The girl had crabs. I had given crabs to my sister. What would Emily Post say? My mind raced to the inevitable thought: Had I also given crabs to my mother? While I shivered at this concept I did get a kick realizing that if I had given them to my mother I had probably also given them to her sleazy cheat-face divorce attorney, which then led me to realize that I had in all likelihood given crabs to Phil's innocent benefit-throwing wife and mother of six who was probably pawing her crotch on a ski lift in Vail while Julia and I shopped for Christmas presents. I was trying not to scratch in front of Julia. If she had gotten them I didn't want her to know from whom.

"I'm going home to take a shower. I'm totally grimy and . . . itchy," she said.

After Mom split that night, Julia and I ordered in burritos and called VideoRoom, Mom's video place on Third Avenue that delivered as well as picked up your videos. Despite this free service, we never managed to get a single video back on time. Delivery was an important feature of our new post-suburban lives. Delivery and twenty-four-hour Korean delis. We thought these urban amenities were symbols of Manhattan, they represented the new "Mom" and, by default, the new "us." We were city people now, kids of divorce, and as such we didn't cook, we ordered in or went out. When the Video-Room guy buzzed I begged Julia to get the door because they always sent this guy from Purchase who worked there on school breaks who had a crush on me, but Julia had a sort of no-bullshitting policy that forbade her to fake anything. She thought you should just be completely forthright all the time. Anything else was phony.

The burritos were good. We had seen the movie before, the butter-meets-girl romantic comedy *Last Tango in Paris,* and it held up as a pleasant way to pass an evening. While we were eating and watching the movie I periodically asked Julia to pass the butter. She fell for it the first time.

In *Last Tango in Paris*, Marlon Brando forbids his young French lover to tell him her name, not her last name, like in an AA kind of way, but her first name. The thing is a steamfest, not the kind of movie best savored with your sullen, mono-syllabic sister. I polished off my burrito, drained my Corona with lime, fluffed my pillow against the bed, itched my rowdy pubes as discreetly as I could manage with Julia sitting a foot away from me in a pastel chintz chair that looked like Baskin-Robbins had gotten into the upholstery business, and settled in for some fat-old-man-fucking-hot-young-girl fuckfest. At one point, the French girl—NO CHARACTER NAMES!—is stroking Brando's chest as he pretends to be the wolf in "Little Red Riding Hood." She says, "Oh, what a lot of fur you have," and he replies, "The better for you to hide your crabs in." I coughed loudly as soon as I heard this, hoping a loud, distracting sound going in Julia's earlobes would prevent the word "crabs" from entering her ear. Julia itched her crotch, but there was something new in her itching, a sense of her hand being connected to her brain. I tried to douse this hand-mind connection and quick by lighting one of Mom's True Blues and blowing smoke around madly. Julia looked right at me.

"What the fuck—"

"What-what, what the fuck?"

"You gave me crabs."

Julia had been developing some kind of paranoid personality disorder over the last few years, but mathematically paranoiacs will hit the truth every few hundred accusations.

"I gave you what?"

"I have been trying to figure out how I got these things, but I should have known, it's you, isn't it?"

"Look, Jules, I like you, but we never fucked."

"I'm going to fucking kill you."

Julia got up and went into the bathroom. The bathroom light flicked on and she was cursing, stream-of-consciousness style.

I puffed on my True Blue and knew that Christmas was ruined, by someone other than my mother for a change. There was little point in trying to calm Julia once she had gone bananas. I blew a couple smoke rings and thought about how there wasn't all that much smoking in *Tango* for a film shot in Paris. I thought the scene in the bathroom where he says he wants her to fuck a pig and then have the pig vomit in her face and her eat it might be coming up. "You're going to miss the part with the 'dying farts of the pig,' Jules. Julia!" I yelled.

"Get in here!" she screamed from the bathroom. "Oh my God!" she screamed. "Bugs! Look at them! Come here, Jeanne."

I took a drag of my cigarette and went into the bathroom. I tossed my cigarette in the toilet. She had placed a pube on the edge of the sink.

"Look at it." She yanked our mother's magnifying mirror, which was attached to the wall, downward and held it over the pube. "Look at it."

"Yeah, yeah. Pubic louse. Real nasty fuckers."

"You're a real dick, Jeanne."

"I thought I had gotten rid of them. I used RID like seven times before I left Purchase."

"I had sex with Mark last night, Jeanne. I probably gave him these things."

"I know. And tonight he's probably giving them to someone else. I'm sorry, Jules. I gave them to Martin, if that makes you feel any better."

"Who'd you get them from?"

"Maggie. She's kind of the root carrier here, the Typhoid Mary of crabs."

I busted out my RID like champagne on a ski trip and we lathered ourselves up. I checked the clock in the kitchen to time ten minutes. I went back to Mom's bedroom where Julia stood in a gray T-shirt with her crotch all soapy with chemicals. When I walked in she angrily lit one of Mom's cigarettes and smoked without acknowledging me. For the next ten minutes we stood, half naked, in Mom's bedroom, finally getting to the scene where the really very lovely French girl sticks two fingers up Brando's ass, an ass I couldn't help feeling might accommodate more than just two digits, while she says she will fuck pigs for him and smell their pig farts. I finally understood what all the film majors at Purchase meant when they touted European filmmakers higher aesthetic and artistic sensibility. At nine forty-four I announced our ten minutes were up. The woman I had spoken with earlier at the Centers for Disease Control in Atlanta had said that unhatched eggs can hatch seven to ten days after the actual crab is killed. I probably needed to do the RID treatment again, since the whole life cycle had started over now that Julia had them. I had now ruined two relationships on account of these wingless bloodsuckers. As I threw the towel in the hamper I realized it was not one of my towels from school, it was one of my mother's and I realized I had used it the day before as well. Big whoops. I grabbed all the towels and threw them in the hamper, vowing to get up early the next day and do laundry.

I didn't even want to think about what Mom would say if she got wind of this whole crab thing, not to mention if we actually gave them to her. I could practically hear her calling Aunt Carol in St. Louis at two in the morning: she would start off crying about the divorce she wanted, which was now a reality. My mom dumped my dad and then wanted people to feel sorry for her. A look-what-I've-done-to-me kind of logic that few people appreciated. Then she'd move on to how her sister Ruth was mean to her on the horse circuit, how there was never enough money, how she was no longer twenty-one, how no one helped her with the housework, how she had had to listen to my father talk about F. Scott Fitzgerald for twenty years. "And now the girls have given me crabs, Carol. I mean, honestly."

And then I overslept the next morning and forgot about the towels. I rushed around finishing my Christmas shopping and then it was time to go out for Christmas Eve dinner, which was our first holiday dinner at a restaurant, with Kitty and a friend of my mother's from Lenox Hill detox, an idea everyone thought was depressing except my mother. Katharine and Eleanor, who were living close by on the Upper East Side since graduating from college, were in the apartment when I got back.

"Why are we going to some dumb restaurant on Christmas Eve?" Katharine asked as Mom strolled around her bedroom in her black stockings, black bra and heels, smoking.

"Dumb? Café des Artistes is hardly dumb. Wait until you see the murals of nymphs on the walls. And the food is fabulous. It's very elegant, Katharine. We're hardly roughing it tonight."

"But we always open up one present on Christmas Eve, after dinner."

"Well, then, Kate, we can open one present at the restaurant."

"What if someone gives you something embarrassing, like a big dildo?"

"I am just trying to have a nice Christmas here, girls."

Once Mom said these words, anything could happen.

I stared at the murals at Café des Artistes through dinner. Since when does my mother have a thing for nymphs? Suddenly our family can't live without nymphs? Our father was probably having a burger alone at the Corner Bistro, talking up some bewildered Danish thirtyish nanny, most likely with a fair degree of success, and our mother's fantastic bombalooed cuisine was now being prepared by some coke-addled '80s power chef. I drank red wine and scratched my pooter under the table. Why I was still itching after doing so many rounds of RID with Martin and then again with Julia was unclear. Maggie was an awfully big slut—perhaps she had given me the super-slut kind of crabs?

Back at Gissy Towers, Mom headed into her bedroom where she made a few failed attempts to reach Phil Sully at home. I hated Phil Sully—he had dopey '50s-looking black hair that looked greased down, like Jim Lehrer. And he was boring like Jim Lehrer, but he wasn't benevolent and kind like Jim Lehrer; he was underhanded and two-timing, a cheat and a fucker. Maybe that is what Jim Lehrer is like, too, but I just don't get that feeling. Mom was sobbing in her bedroom, and you could hear her flipping pages in her address book, looking for someone to call in St. Louis, where it was an hour earlier, to cry to about her horrible life. I was sorry she didn't manage to get Phil Sully on the horn.

"I'm itching like crazy," Julia barked, pawing at the crotch of her charcoal wool skirt.

I started taking the pillows off the pull-out couch. "Yeah, well, maybe that stuff wasn't fresh. That pharmacy's kind of for old people. They probably don't get crabs too much so maybe the medicine was expired."

"We'll sleep on the floor tonight." She lit a cigarette as if she had just come up with a diabolical plan that couldn't be more airtight. She sat in the big pastel striped chair smoking. Julia was a person who fanned her own cigarette, as if someone else's smoking were bothering her. She alternately puffed and fanned in an exasperated manner.

"Jesus Christ, awful," she said. I watched her nonsmoker and smoker battle it out for a minute and wondered whether any Darst had been diagnosed as having a split personality.

"What—" I said, reaching for Mom's cigarettes on the coffee table. True Blue was a smoke you endured only if you were out of cigs or too drunk to care. I tore the plastic cylindrical filter off, making it a little less like smoking some old lady's vagina. "—are you talking about?" I blew a couple of smoke rings, a skill I wished at that moment were somehow in demand, as I didn't know what else I was good at or would do once college was over.

"We've still got these things, Jeanne. Don't you see that sleeping on the pull-out—that's just gonna keep infesting the pull-out. And then what the fuck are we gonna do?" I considered the word "infestating." It didn't sound right. But you couldn't bring these matters up with Julia. She was too volatile for grammar talk. She'd get up and do something bonkers, like grab scissors and give you bangs in the back of your head. "We'll get something stronger tomorrow but until then, we're not infestating the pull-out."

"Okay, fine." I put out my cigarette. There was a plushy carpet to sleep on, so it could have been worse. I got the pillows, blankets and comforters out of the hall closet, resigned to slave mode for the remainder of the break. We got in our little homemade beds on the floor and said nothing. Mom's room was now quiet as well. All through the house not a creature was stirring, not even a dual-diagnosis depressive-alcoholic. But nighttime was the busy time for the buggers living in my crotch.

The next morning Mom came out and found us in two rectangular piles on her living room floor.

"What are you girls doing?" She stood over me, a cigarette in one hand and a coffee in the other.

"Trying to sleep," Julia snapped from under the covers.

I rustled my feet out from under the little blanket trap they were in.

"I can see that. Why are you on the floor? Did you girls break my pull-out? That's a very expensive couch I'll have you know."

"Jeanne has crabs. And she gave them to me," came from under Julia's pile across the room.

"What?" Mom said, pulling at her cigarette.

"Nothing. Nothing. She's kidding." I threw one of my heels at Julia.

"What did she say?" Mom asked.

"Nothing. She's kidding around."

"So why are you girls on the floor? I thought you said the pull-out was very comfortable."

"It is. We just were too drunk to pull it out last night."

"No we weren't." Julia pushed the blankets off herself abruptly and sat up. "Jeanne got crabs and gave them to me."

"Oh, for God's sake, Jeanne. You've got lice?"

"Yeah, but they're in our pubes," Julia said.

"This is what you get for going to a state school, Jeanne. Why you couldn't get in somewhere decent I'll never understand. You're so bright."

"Mom, I didn't get them at Purchase. Maggie gave them to me over Thanksgiving."

"Honestly," Mom said, going to the kitchen. I glared at Julia.

"Thanks a lot."

"No, thank you. Fucking carrier."

Doris came back into the room. "Now, who wants some coffee? It's Gevalia. It's Swiss."

I got up, taking my pile of blankets in my arms, and headed for the bathroom. I stopped at the hall closet and opened the door. Julia was behind me.

"What are you doing? Please tell me you're not putting those back in there! We've got to quarantine all bedding and blankets. Go get some garbage bags from the kitchen," she ordered. We bagged up all our bedding from the previous night and shoved it into the closet, took showers and reconvened in the living room.

Doris was doing the *New York Times* crossword when we came back in and sat with our coffees. I don't know why I expected to smell something coming out of the kitchen—I was having a Pavlovian moment, I guess—but I did. Bacon maybe, or those baked eggs in the ramekins with the olive oil and rosemary and oregano and Parmesan cheese on top she used to make. The lack of bedrooms was new, but the complete absence of food I had seen before. She stopped cooking for Dad before she left him and now there wasn't even any food in the house ever. Mom was trying to starve us out of her life.

"Merry Christmas, dollies."

"Oh shit, it's Christmas," I said to Julia, "the pharmacy's not going to be open and I doubt any others will be open, either."

"For what?" Mom said, eyes down on her crossword.

"Crab stuff," Julia said loudly, knowing I hated explicitness.

"Oh, for heaven's sake. That again?"

"I used the medicine like six times now," I said, defending myself.

"Six times? Well, then you're fine."

"So why are we still itching?" Julia sipped her coffee. "Anybody want to explain that?" my sister said, seeming to suggest that we had been the victims of foul play.

"You'll have to give the medicine a chance. They're probably in their death throes. I honestly don't want to hear about it again. Can't we just have a nice Christmas?"

Mom's eyes welled up underneath her enormous Yves Saint

Laurent wraparound tortoiseshell glasses, which might have doubled as welding goggles in a woodshop on the Côte d'Azur.

"Yes, yes," I said, hoping to cut her off before she went too far into Divorced Ladyville.

"Is there a Rite Aid on Fourteenth Street?" Julia said.

"No one is going down to Fourteenth Street today. I mean it. I can't take all this silliness. I really can't, girls. Don't push me because I am about ready to have a breakdown here." Mom looked up from her crossword and wiped a tear from under her glasses. Weepylady was back.

"Okay, okay, Mom—easy, champ." I got up and went to her bony shoulders and began to rub them.

"Now, when does school start up again for you girls?"

That night we opened up our presents at Gissy Towers. One by one Eleanor, Katharine, Julia and I unwrapped four black leather miniskirts from Ann Taylor.

"Aren't they adorable?" Mom said. She loved giving presents as much as she liked getting them, no matter how big or small, silly or serious. Besides bulk, her other specialty was presents that only she found funny; the year before, we had all gotten socks that had rhinestones where your toenails would go. ("Can you stand it? I think they're a riot!")

It was unclear whether Mom actually imagined a scene wherein all four of us would wear the black leather miniskirts at the same time, like a Robert Palmer video starring her DNA, but if there was one thing you didn't do if you didn't want Mom to turn into Princess Runningwater before your eyes, it was show anything less than hysterical gratitude over gifts.

The day after Christmas, Julia and I went to the drugstore on the corner of Eighty-sixth and York where Mom had an account and charged some more crab medicine. We also got some thick, black Hefty garbage bags that Julia decided would be good for storing our clothes in when they came back from the laundry place. Mom asked why no one was wearing their new black leather miniskirts.

"We can't risk it, Mom. The adult crabs are now probably dead, after the last treatment, but the eggs, the larvae, can hatch up to seven days after the actual crabs are dead, so it's really too risky," I said.

"And dry-cleaning leather? Forget it. That'd be like fourteen bucks," Julia added, taking off the big lid of the giant pasta pot on the stove to see if the water was boiling. Mom made her way into the small kitchen, scooching by Julia and reaching for the French press near the stove.

"Well, I was going to make some coffee in the French press. It's the absolute best way to make coffee. Who'd like some?"

Julia was focused on slowly lowering hairbrushes like lobsters into a boiling cauldron. There were thin plastic round hairbrushes, like rolling pins with bristles, a wooden flat brush, a tortoiseshell comb and an oval brush. Then Julia began to lower a bunch of silver antique hairbrushes and combs on the end of a slotted spoon into the water. Mom slammed down the half-and-half and brought the tortoiseshell welding goggles that hung around her neck up to her eyes.

"What in God's name are you doing? Those are antique sterling-silver brushes of my mother's! Are you insane?"

"We've been way too lax," Julia said, with no emotion.

"Take those out of there right now. I mean it, Julia. I have had it with this nonsense. You girls have been in this apartment for a week and you're making me nuts. You haven't even used those brushes. They've been sitting on my dresser for forty-five years."

Julia began taking the silver brushes off the spoon.

"Get some plan together for today. Go to the Met or the Whitney. Something. I mean it. I am at my wit's end here."

Mom took her coffee and flew out of the kitchen.

Julia said we were "in the final phase," and we needed one last push to get these things out of our lives forever. We decided to head down to Century 21 and bought some cheapo sheets and blankets we could throw out rather than have to schlep more laundry to the Chinese laundry place. As for our other clothes, we changed Laundromats, since the water obviously wasn't hot enough at the old place to kill these things, bringing bags of clothes that had been washed thirty-one times in seven days to another place seven blocks down York Avenue.

We repoisoned ourselves with new prescription stuff containing lindane, which we got at a free clinic in Harlem, since the stuff from the German pharmacy clearly was defective. The person who examined us said it didn't appear that we still had any crabs but Julia let her know that they were indeed still among us. Not really giving a shit either way, the clinic worker called in a prescription to the pharmacy, and we got "the good stuff" later that afternoon. The old Yorkville German at the pharmacy must have been half a *Gugelhupf* away from calling Doris and letting her know that her pubic lice medicine bill was astronomical this month. Walking up York Avenue, I told Julia this was the last time I was going to slather my poor vag with napalm.

"The lindane bottle instructions said that too many applications could cause intense itching even though the crabs were gone. We don't have them anymore. I don't think we've had them for a while."

She looked both ways before whispering that I was the one who had brought these microscopic pubic gorillas into our lives and she was only trying to get us out of this mess.

I started to answer her but she shushed me as an older woman in a navy-blue quilted coat steered her beagle around the two of us and made a left in front of us.

"The people in this neighborhood are really unbelievable. You gotta keep it down, Jeanne." This is precisely what I was afraid of: the crab medicine seemed to be penetrating Julia's frontal lobe.

"By the way," she added, sotto voce, "make sure you rip off the label on those bottles. I for one don't want my name connected with this whole fiasco." Not realizing Julia was planning on running for public office, I clinched the pharmacy bag to make it unrecognizable as a bag from the pharmacy containing crab medicine while we walked past Mario the doorman into the building.

That night Mom was out with Phil Sully and we did our last "treatment," lathering ourselves from head to toe in soapy poison. We did our crotches, head hair, eyebrows, arms. We shaved our legs and armpits, used depilatory cream on the blond hair on our upper lips. Then we sat on towels watching Tod Browning's *Freaks* while rhythmically pulling our little combs through our tresses and depositing imaginary eggs on a towel in front of us.

"Why did we rent this movie again?" Julia said, sitting on a garbage bag, tapping nonexistent bugs off her little pube comb. "These people are so sad."

After the movie we decided to call it a night. I was tired and had a backache from sleeping on the floor.

"Julia, I think we can sleep on the pull-out tonight. I think we're clear."

She eyeballed me for a few moments. "Fine." She walked out of the room and then came back in, holding two garbage bags. "But we'll seal off our crotches with these," and she handed me a garbage bag. She took a scissors off the desk and cut two holes in her bag. She then stepped into the Hefty bag holes and pulled the bag up around her waist. "Now all this needs is a little belt." Julia left the room and went into the kitchen. Too tired to argue, I cut two holes in my bag and pulled it on.

"Okay. Got it," Julia said, coming back into the room. "Check it out, better than a belt, that would be uncomfortable to sleep in." She shoved her hip at me where there was now gray duct tape.

She waddled over to the coffee table in her big plastic garbage-bag diaper and pulled a True Blue out of a pack sitting on the table. She lit it and sat on a chair.

"See? You can sit anywhere, too. We should have been wearing these the whole time," Julia said, handing me the duct tape. She took a little drag. "God, these things are disgusting. Smoking is disgusting, you know that?"

I took off my T-shirt and duct-taped the bag together with a depressive's flair. I went to take a piss in just my garbage bag.

As I walked back into the now darkened living room, the front door opened, blasting voices and light. My mother and a man. The golfy bellow of a lawyer. Before I could grab a blanket to cover my chest, Mom flicked on more lights. Mom and Phil Sully, both totally drunk, stood at the door. Julia was asleep in her bra and garbage bag on the pull-out. I was standing, frozen. I grabbed a needlepoint Picasso pillow off a chair and covered my breasts, and before I knew it my manners kicked in and I stuck out my hand.

"Hi, Mr. Sully."

Mr. S. shook my hand and took in my getup.

"Jeanne, nice to see you again," he managed to eject out the side of his little lawyer mouth.

"Girls, what in God's name is going on here? What are you wearing? Oh, for God's sake." If she hadn't been totally bombed she would have really been pissed. Being so drunk, though, she was about forty percent open to something happening that was not what her eyes told her was happening. Julia continued to sleep, despite the light, the conversation, the scotch vapors emanating from my mother and her boyfriend like dirt off Pig-Pen. Mom objected to every guy Julia had ever dated, and yet Julia had never taken a married divorce lawyer to the fall Sports Dance at the Bronxville Field Club.

"Jeanne, go get some clothes on."

"Nice to see you again, Mr. Sully," I mumbled as I slunk off, toward Mom's bedroom.

I came out after I heard the door closing. Mom was sitting in a chair, smoking.

"Well, that was quite a display," Mom said, and she went into her bedroom without saying good night.

I had a hard time falling asleep; each turn in my garbage bag gaucho made a noisy, crinkly sound, reawakening me and reminding me of the clingy creatures that seemingly wouldn't go away, creatures that may or may not still exist, I didn't know anymore, bugs, things that passed from one person to another. Mom didn't believe we still had them, if she ever believed we had them in the first place. Why couldn't we get rid of them? I could hear Mom yelling and then laughing and then crying to somebody on the phone. I got up and opened the window. I was hot, though it was January 5. The bag made my legs feel clammy and sweaty. I wondered whether I was losing any of my freshman fifteen in all this, not that I really cared.

To get out of Mom's hair, so to speak, Julia and I went to Bronxville the next day to see some high school friends. As the train pulled out of Grand Central, Julia gave me a few orders.

"Do not sleep at Maggie's tonight," she said, sipping a sugary Zabar's coffee. "I like her and everything, but she's a slut and she gave us crabs."

"Maggie's not a slut, Julia. She's an alcoholic."

"Well, she didn't get crabs from a bottle of tequila. That's a worm in the bottle, not a crab."

"Okey-doke, Jules. Can we talk about something else? I'm trying to block out the garbage bag rash I now have all over my inner thighs."

Julia leaned into me. "Could you please keep it down, Jeanne? God. Don't you think these Bronxville businessmen would love to pass on a nice crab tale starring the Darst girls to their daughters at dinner tonight?"

The conductor came around and punched our tickets, sliding them in the backs of our seats, a practice I have never fully understood. It just seems like fake work. We agreed to meet on the NY side platform for the nine-o'clock train back Saturday.

When we got back to Mom's on Saturday night we came in quietly. We had gone to Bronxville to see friends as much as to stave off a hissy fit from Mom. We had made it through Christmas break. We would be going back to school tomorrow and for once Mom hadn't had her annual Christmas meltdown.

There was no sound coming from her bedroom, strange considering it wasn't that late and the light was on. Julia looked at me and shrugged her shoulders, turning into the bathroom. I stood outside Mom's bedroom. The worst thing one could do at this point in the night was to engage Mom, unless you wanted to hear about how she fell out of her bedroom window at eleven and was sidelined from the Lexington Junior League Horse Show, the most important twelve-and-under equestrian event in the country, but since I was leaving the next day for school and we had really pissed her off with the whole Phil Sully/garbage bag thing, I decided to go in and say good night.

I opened the door and Mom was lying facedown in the ivory-colored carpet. The rug around her head was red and black. I went to her and pulled her up by her shoulders as well as I could, her head drooping forward and gushing blood onto my T-shirt and jeans. I called out to Julia. She phoned 911. They told me to apply pressure to where her head was spurting blood until the ambulance got there, which was within about four minutes. They took her to Doctors Hospital around the corner. We walked the block and a half there ourselves, rather than get in the ambulance. I had a lot of blood on my shirt and hands. We spent most of the night talking to doctors, who said she would be okay but would have died if we had not gone in her room until the morning. There was also a social worker who took her alcohol history from us. (It was either eight or nine rehabs she had been to at this point, we couldn't remember.) We called Eleanor and Katharine but they did not come that night. Mom was handled in shifts by this time. They would come in the morning. They would take it from there. We were all so close in age, there was never a feeling of we're older, we'll take care of this, this is the thing to do with Doris. They were more competent and responsible than Julia and I were, yes. But no one could handle Doris. Not us, not my dad, not her friends, not her shrinks, AA, married boyfriends. People were never called to come and rectify the situation. People were called to give other people breaks. They would check her into Lenox Hill detox again or some other rehab. We should go back to school.

Leaving the emergency wing, walking down East End Avenue with Mom's watch of Nonnie's and her wedding rings and diamond earrings in our jeans pockets, Julia and I walked in silence, bleary, blood on our shirts and jeans, having no idea what time it was. It seemed crazy, but I wondered whether we should have asked the doctors to check our mother for crabs.

PAINTERS ON BICYCLES

EVERYONE AT PURCHASE had artistic purpose. They were painters, actors, opera singers, classical musicians, film directors, dancers. They were there to become artists. I was there because I was an academic fuck-up, which, thankfully, looks a lot like being an artist.

It was conceived and built as New York's state art school, the artsy child of the SUNY (State University of New York) system. The campus itself looked like a prison during a drought. The buildings were brown brick—rumored to have been donated by Governor Nelson Rockefeller's construction business—low and drab. Construction began in 1967, and as it went on, it seemed that Purchase chose Kent State as its muse, adding features such as an underground tunnel system so no students could take over a building, and giving the dorm rooms about six inches of space under the doors so campus police could throw tear bombs in and smoke out rioters. Cheery stuff.

In an upside-down collegiate universe, the arts departments

were first-rate and difficult to get into, while the other departments had all the cache of a community college. So Humanities students were the losers at Purchase. History, Psychology, Math, Science? Scram. I have a movie to cast. Many of the students had gone to The High School for the Performing Arts in Manhattan, the "*Fame* school," but I didn't see much dancing on cabs while I was there. While I was used to being around kids who were smart and driven, they were driven out of some robotic obligation to be rich like their parents. The students at Purchase were making art, films, studying opera singing because they wanted to, because they loved these things. I met all kinds of interesting people there. But that doesn't mean they knew how to drink.

The first weekend there I looked around and realized I was living with three other girls. Just like home. Why did everyone else seem so excited? My roommate and the two girls in the other room of our suite let it be known they liked to party. One evening the whole gang came bounding into my room and announced their devilish intentions.

"There's a social in the Humanities building and we're gonna get some wine coooolers! You wanna party?"

With three four-packs of Bartles & Jaymes? I think not. I don't want to be stuck with a case of alcoholic blue-balls when you ladies run out of wine coolers and pass out and I can't get anything else to drink. No way.

———

MY SECOND YEAR I was assigned a roommate in this on-campus apartment and it turned out I was going to be living with someone from an equally no-fun-to-drink-with category, a religious group called "the Believers." I have no idea what church they were from but the Believers were always starting a very caring conversation with you. "Hi. How are you today?" and it would always end with "Well, you should come to a Bible study we're having this Friday!" which was so shocking to me. Here we are, having a gay old time while waiting for our horrible food, holding our horrible green plastic trays side by side at this horrible cafeteria at this horrible little college and you spring this shit on me? Bible study? I thought we were making a connection here! Do you have any idea how much you have fucked my shit up now?

My believing roommate was a four-foot black girl named Mindy. Mindy was unfailingly upbeat, smiley and energetic. I tried to be nice to Mindy even though she was unfailingly upbeat, smiley and energetic, snored disproportionately loudly to her body weight (my guess is eighty pounds) and took to calling me by a nickname that my father and only my father has called me for my entire life, Jean-Joe.

"Hey, Jean-Joe, what's shakin'?"

"You need anything from the grocery store, Jean-Joe?"

"You feel like praying before we turn out the light, Jean-Joe?"

Someone like this wouldn't last two minutes in my life

now, but at that point I was convinced she'd see herself to the door, probably by failing out of school since she spent every second running around organizing ways to trick students into accidentally stumbling onto the Bible study on Friday nights instead of ever cracking a book. When she wasn't out "spreadin' it!" Mindy was on our couch watching a children's game show that featured a lot of pie-throwing and water-gun fights.

I was dating an actor, the pinnacle of the Purchase caste system, and after a lot of dry humping on couches it was time to put this show on its feet and see what was what. A long weekend was upon us and I planned on going away with Mike. Mindy was headed home to the Bronx. After she caught a ride into the city with another Believer, I packed a bag in the very quiet, now prayer-free room of ours. I noticed an envelope on my bed. I picked it up and it said "Jean-Joe" on the front. I expected some kind of uplifting weekend message. "God's on your team, kid!" or the classic "God loves you!" but it said none of these chirpy, miniature Mindyisms. It read, in very small print, in dark pencil: "You are about to sleep with the devil." This was heavy even for Mindy.

Had Mindy slept with Mike? Did this mean Mike was good or bad in the sack? I had to think that in Mindy's world this meant neither. It meant that Mike was a devil and that sex was evil. Or maybe, more interestingly, sex with actors was evil? If that's what the cryptic warning meant I should have listened. The sex with Mike turned out to be a major non-event. In the theater when a show is about to start and there's hardly anyone in the audience, the rule is: if the cast is larger than the audience, you can cancel the show. There should be some kind of similar rule for women who see a small penis. If my vagina is bigger than your cock, everybody's going home. Sorry folks. No show tonight. See you next time.

When I realized there would be no real drinking at this school I turned to the only thing I could think of doing with the hand that wasn't smoking: I wrote papers, read the assigned books, went to classes. I liked my journalism class a lot, which was a shock because I never considered doing the work that my grandmother and grandfather and my father and my cousin did. I retired from journalism quickly, however, and started to write short stories. While college was just a blackout-sex, alcohol-soaked free-for-all for most people I knew from Bronxville, I barely drank at college. Not that I didn't occasionally explode and drink my face off. I did. I just mean, for me, I hardly drank at all. For someone normal, I drank quite a bit.

AT MY CAMPUS JOB, I met Carmen. We hated each other from the top. I sometimes feel this is a barometer for how much I will care for someone: Do I hate your guts the first time I meet you? If yes, we're probably destined for a long and meaningful relationship. I was still working in the cage at the gym, handing out towels to horny businessmen from nearby PepsiCo, one of the school's major sponsors for the arts, when

Carmen came in for her shift. She stormed in, her boyfriend, Sal, not far behind her. She was late (there was a "latemotif" to her life) and she was angry. Anger was really not an emotion in Carmen's life story. It was the plot. Sal followed her into the cage, the area we worked in, so well named. She then got in a fight with a PepsiCo executive who wanted the little arty freaks to smile when we handed him his towel. George, our boss, tried to put his managerial touch on the whole fiasco. But you didn't tell Carmen what to do, even if you employed her. She yelled at George, too, and was fired.

I HAD NEVER SEEN this kind of workaday theatricality. My mother's drama was a pity-pot, little-rich-girl version. Carmen was Hispanic and loud and ghetto and funny. In Westchester, and in whitey culture in general, there's a premium placed on manners, civility, pleasantries, particularly among women. Carmen didn't operate *comme ça*. I was impressed. She was not as taken with me. Someone down the hall had done my hair in cornrows the night before. I wasn't trying to be black or Bo, I was just stoned. Carmen took one look at me as she packed up her work things for good and said, "Who did your hair?"

"Karen, this girl down the hall."

"Umm hmm. Where you live?"

"My mom lives on Eighty-seventh and York."

"Umm hmm."

"What about you?"

"Ninety-seventh and Amsterdam. The West Side, honey," she said, and shot me a threatening look.

I thought that was probably it. There would be no halfway point where we'd meet between our two houses. After that day we'd never see each other again. But shortly after she was canned from the gym, I ran into her at the library where she was now working, and she needed a roommate desperately. I saw an opportunity to get away from the littlest Believer and I took it. A few weeks after living together I convinced Carmen to write a show of skits and stand-up comedy and improvisation.

Carmen was mad at me all the time. This was our schtick: passionate Latina and bumbling white lady, and like a lot of schticks it was our real life, too. She was mad at me because I drank too much, was impossibly white and suburban and rich (which I was, relative to her), fancy and carefree, which she saw as inane. I was messy, didn't clean a whole lot, prompting lots of "Just 'cause I'm dark don't mean I'm gonna scrub the bathroom!" routines. She didn't understand extreme drunkenness and blacking out. I tried to explain that this is what civilized people do, but she couldn't make the cultural leap. What I ate drove her crazy. "You just put a little tomato and mayonnaise and salt and pepper on a couple pieces of bread—it's delicious."

"No. No, you can't! That's insane! You need some meat on there or it's not a sandwich!"

"Yes it is. It's called a tomato sandwich. I'm going to make you one."

"I'm not gonna eat it."

One night I got drunk and she was a little drunk and I suggested we go down on each other. She went berserk and told me to fuck off, but I kept pestering her. "It'll be fun! Come on! Let's just try it." A "Take one big bite" kind of argument, like you'd have with a three-year-old about spinach.

Finally she got on board and we went in the bedroom. She went first, and I thought she did a good job, it wasn't really my thing but it was an experience. For someone who had to be convinced she certainly gave it a thorough go. Then it was my turn to do her. Well, the booze was starting to wear off and frankly the idea was losing its luster. Then I was confronted with the actual female anatomy, and man, I was not feeling good about this. I did my best and came up with some creative ways to get through it, when Carmen stopped me and said, "What are you doing?"

"I'm, um, you know, eating you out."

"No you're not. What is that, is that the blanket? Are you using the blanket on my pussy instead of your mouth?"

"No! No. I just had to—"

"You're not even doing it. You're pretending. You're pretending to eat me out. I did you! I swear to God, Jeanne!"

"I'm sorry. It's just, it's really gross and I can't do it. I was doing it, though. I was."

Carmen threw me out of our room for the next few nights. I guess it was a classic case of unrequited cunnilingus, and we never talked about it again. I felt the same way about writing our show together. She would pretend to be writing but I was doing most of it, I was the one doing all the work. And most of the time I was perfectly happy doing all the work. Writing our show, writing, seemed like something I might want to do with myself.

After living with Dad for twenty-three years, my mother certainly wasn't going to jump for joy that I wanted to write; my sisters didn't care, as long as I didn't TALK about writing.

I had always had my heart set on doing nothing, but play-writing came along and I thought, Why not? I'd like to take a few precautions not to go insane and die broke, chatting with wallpaper like my grandmother did and whatnot, but other than that, could it be so bad? When Dad found out that I was doing some playwriting and poetry and short stories he called me at my mother's apartment one weekend and said he was driving to Rye to a dinner party and "why don't I give you a ride back to Purchase and we'll talk about whether you should try and get a job at a small paper somewhere, à la Hemingway, it's the best way to get used to writing every day."

I accepted the ride back to school. I spotted his little red Dodge Omni coming toward me up York Avenue and saw there were other people in the car. I hopped in and introduced to some ("very interesting gal, hell of a nice guy, used to write for *The Nation* . . . ") people. I don't know why I thought there wouldn't be a couple of "terrific-looking" Austrian novelists in the car with my dad. It started to rain right around the curve of the Willis Avenue Bridge but Dad remained focused on something he was saying rather than something he was driving. I barely noticed but the Austrian in the backseat with me was clearly terrified. It was a stormy, curvy, windows-up, oxygen-deprived, harrowing monologue of a ride with no say whatsoever in your own safety or well-being or the topic of conversation so yeah, I was utterly at home. They dropped me off and drove off in the storm.

The next day my mother called. "I suppose you've heard what happened with your father."

"No."

"Apparently after he dropped you off he drove down some stairs and couldn't get back up the stairs. I'm not sure. There were some Austrian writers who were coming out of the library. Sounds like the blind leading the blind, if you ask me."

"The Austrians were *in* the car. What steps?" I realized the only steps my mother could be talking about were the library steps. My father had driven down this long set of stairs that is not wide, really, just a regular person staircase, not like the steps up the Jefferson Memorial or anything, and he would have had to have driven from my apartment onto the mall, a brick esplanade kind of thing meant, again, for pedestrians to get around, not cars. I had never seen a car on the mall ever. So he drove onto the mall like someone in a Jerry Bruckheimer movie, and then went down this narrow staircase where he landed in front of the library. Again, a place where cars didn't go because there was no way for them to get there. I called him up.

"God damn it, Jean-Joe, I know it's a state school and all,

but do you think they might have a little something in the budget for a few signs here and there?"

"Signs? Dad, there's a road and then the road ends. What kind of sign do you want?"

"Well, I'll tell ya, some damn nice kids helped me push my car back up those stairs but it must've made the Austrians a little nervous. They took the train back to the city, which I thought was a little unnecessary."

I wasn't looking forward to hearing around campus about the lunatic who had driven down the library steps, but at the same time I was glad to have avoided a conversation with him about writing. The last time we'd talked I'd told him I might major in African-American literature, and his reaction was calm, measured, as if trying to get me to move a knife away from my own throat.

"Now, Jeanne, hold on a minute, hold on here. I can see your attraction, particularly to James Baldwin and so forth, there's no doubt Maya Angelou is terrific, God, and Zora Neale Hurston, really terrific. But at some point the black experience is just one experience, while majoring in, let's say, European literature, opens up so many other experiences, the big ones, ones you can tackle right now, with the benefit of good professors and your peers. You may never get that chance again. That's all I'm saying. Think it over. Give it a day or two and we'll talk." His reaction to my wanting to write could turn into a real box set. It would start with what books I should read on writing ("Gardner's terrific, of course, but no one can top Frank O'Connor's *The Lonely Voice* on the short story, now let's see, I assume you've read Cather's book on writing already? Updike's essays are in themselves lessons in writing, have you ever tried John Middleton Murry on style? You can't forget F. R. Leavis on the novel. I'm going to photocopy some Keats for ya, because you just can't get better lessons than from just reading Keats. You'll learn more from the poets simply because there's more critical writing on poetry. Prose has only been taken seriously since about 1850 . . .") and go on and on and on from there.

A LITERATURE PROFESSOR at SUNY Purchase named Bell Chevigny was the advisor on our senior project, the two-woman show that Carmen and I wrote and performed. Bell had just written a novel and she invited us to her apartment around Riverside and 110th for a book party. She gave us an inscribed copy of her new novel. Was there anything cooler? I was friends with someone whose book was published, a woman, someone who was happily married and had two daughters. Carmen liked Bell quite a bit, we both did, but Bell was an important symbol for me, a happy, successful writer with a family and many friends who was not living in poverty. Bell wasn't a drunk, either. A mother. A writer. A normal person.

Our two-woman show, *This Side of Virginity*, a play on the title of Fitzgerald's first novel, *This Side of Paradise*, was a big hit, got a great review in that journalistic knockout of a student newspaper, *The Load*. We were on our way, like the acting students, the dancers everybody wanted to fuck, the painters who rode around on vintage bikes in jeans splattered in multicolored oils, the ultra-focused film majors, to artistic superiority. I thought we'd hit *Saturday Night Live* to start off with and then I would bust out a humor piece in *The New Yorker*, establishing me as an incredibly hilarious serious writer. The movies and plays I would do would insure I could travel as much as I wanted and not have to work jobs to support the precarious writing life. Unlike my father, I had a backup plan, a plan B as they say. Acting. I'd like to reiterate in case you missed that: Acting was my backup career, my safety net so that I wouldn't have to be broke.

Dad came to our show and loved it and called every other day with ideas for Carmen and me and our next show. He thought it'd be great if we did a parody of William F. Buckley's TV show, *Firing Line*. Carmen didn't even know what that was, and I tried to explain to Dad the utter lunacy of a twenty-year-old Dominican woman playing William F. Buckley while I took on the role of John Kenneth Galbraith. *Meet the Press* was another show he thought we'd be terrific at parodying.

He'd leave messages on our answering machine. "Jean, it's Dad. I got an idea for you. I got an idea for you, I got an idea for Carmen . . ."

A FAILED DIVORCE

AT FIRST THEY ACTED like normal divorced people. They were angry and they spoke badly of one another and dated other people and not each other. Mom could actually smell our father on us when we came in the door on Sunday night after a weekend at his place.

"Have you been at your father's? You reek of franks and beans." He was renting his friend Quig's house in Springs, Long Island, and the wood-burning stove there, the "black cat" as his neighbor the artist Saul Steinberg called it, did leave you smelling as if you had been camping. That first Thanksgiving they were divorced she forbade him to enter her apartment, so Dad took us to a sushi place on Third Avenue, not a "Calvin Trillin Chinatown dumpling house on Thanksgiving" kind of place, but rather a last-minute "Dad didn't make a reservation anywhere" kind of place. The place was empty, aka totally depressing and potentially gastro-disastrous. My dad was not a big sushi person but the man would eat anything; he had a tendency to finish everything on his plate and then reach toward yours.

"Are you going to eat that piece of mackerel there, Jean-Joe?" my dad said, hand poised above the piece of fish on my plate, suspended like a giant white-man hand puppet, awaiting my answer.

"Umm, no."

"I didn't think you had plans for that one," he said, popping it into his mouth. "Now, tell me, Jean, reading any of the English poets? I mean the greats. Keats? Blake? Who've you tried?" and before I could answer, my dad had spread wasabi on the green plastic separator things that act as some kind of plate decoration and lobbed it into his mouth and began chomping on it.

"Dad! Jesus Christ!" Katharine yelled. "That's a *garnis!*"

"A what?" my dad said with wide eyes, as if he had eaten a blowfish.

"A *garnis!* It's plastic. Decoration. You're not supposed to eat it!" Eleanor said, looking around to see if the waitstaff was watching. My dad pulled the green plastic matter from his mouth and laid it on his empty plate.

That Thanksgiving was the last time he ever took us out to dinner. He'd run out of his house money. That piece of mackerel was the official start of destitute divorced dad.

He was early to pick us up for Christmas. Ever since I can remember, my father never had anywhere else he had to be.

He was sitting on one of the couches in the lobby with a bag of presents on either side of his knees. He wore a hat;

he still bought and wore hats, mostly from this prehistoric preppy store on Madison and Forty-sixth, F. R. Tripler. Tripler's was his only charge account, so you could count on some things from there at Christmas. The men's section may have been passable, but the women's clothes were the most outdated, buttoned-up, queer shit imaginable. What old money wear in menopause.

He got up and gave his usual huge greeting. "Jean-Joe! Eleanora! Julita! Katarina! Mer-ry Christmas! Sit. Sit. Have I got some great things for you all." My dad, hat and gray overcoat still on, began taking presents out of the bags, all unwrapped. My father had never wrapped a present ever. It totally threw off your timing as the person getting the gift because you could plainly see what you were being given as he reached across people to hand it to you and out of politeness you had to maintain a façade of suspense as he passed the unclothed gift your way. There were biographies he got half-price at the Strand, a button-down shirt with a silk tie at the collar from Tripler's that Pat Buckley might wear to jury duty, and then the worst kind of present my dad gave—an expensive item, like a fancy camera that you knew meant he wasn't going to eat for a week.

We sat in the lobby opening presents, thankful that because Mom was new to the building we didn't know any of the people coming and going to their holiday festivities, passing us and giving the raised eyebrow to the doorman, Mario. Katharine and Eleanor, the two people in our family who had incomes, entry-level though they were, made a couple overtures to actually going somewhere for brunch, but Dad cheerfully dismissed these wacky notions.

"Oh, I think we're good right here. What do you think about that *OED*, Jean-Joe? There's a manual that comes with it on how to use it and also a magnifying glass, which, even at your age, you're going to need, believe me. Oh, it's wonderful. Your life as you know it? Gone, I'm telling ya. You'll thank me later."

"Thanks, Dad."

"You're very welcome."

My father then reached into one of his bags and pulled out a large hunk of Parmesan cheese.

"I thought my bio of Rebecca West smelled a little funny." Katharine giggled.

"Murray's cheese shop on Bleecker." He pulled a knife out of his herringbone overcoat and chiseled off a flaky hunk. "Eleanor? Can I interest you in some of the finest of Parma?"

Eleanor, on the verge of tears, uttered, "No thank you."

"All right, then, terrible decision but you are free to make it. Katarina?"

"Sure. Yummy." He handed Katharine the crumbly cheese.

"Help yourself to some of that good bread. Now, who else would like a bit? Julia, what's the name of the doorman again?"

"Mario, but he doesn't want any cheese, Dad," Julia said.

"Nonsense. It's Christmas and he's working. Where's your spirit?"

"Please don't offer him any cheese, Dad," Eleanor pleaded.

"What is wrong with you girls?" My dad stood up and then yelled across the lobby, "Mario! Mario!"

Mario put his *Daily News* down.

"Can I interest you in some of the finest Parmesan this side of the Mediterranean?"

"Oh no, thank you, sir."

"You're not being polite, are you, Mario?"

"Dad, he doesn't want any cheese," I said.

"Okay, I will have some. Thank you."

"Terr-ific. Okay, let's see here . . ." And my dad began jabbing at the Parmesan with his knife again. "Where are you from, Mario?"

"Italy."

"What part?" My dad placed a chunk of cheese in Mario's palm.

"Umbria."

"Umbria, my God, that's gorgeous land! Your family farmers or winemakers or what?" My dad nibbled on a bit of cheese as if he were at a cocktail party in Southampton.

Just then the doors of one of the two elevators opened and Mom and Phil Sully got out. Mom's eyes went to the cheese on the lobby table, the presents everywhere, the crumbly baguette on the table, Dad, Mario and us girls. While it didn't reflect favorably on Dad, it wasn't what you'd call a moment of glory for Mom or Phil Sully, either. Mr. Sully probably wouldn't want the New York Bar Association knowing he was dating a client. Mom simply walked through it like a rain shower.

"Steve. Girls." Mario trotted to the door and held it for them as they walked out of the lobby into the sharp December chill and Eighty-seventh Street.

My father didn't miss a beat. "Katarina, I am about two weeks away from all my Fitzgerald research being done. Did I tell you that? I wish to hell that I could find that he once ran into a blaze and pulled out an orphan. Jesus, the more you know, the more difficult it is to like the guy."

Dad's divorced-dad game was strong: impromptu passes made at cashiers at the IGA in Amagansett with whom we had gone to grade school, amorous lunges at Julia's college friend's older sister out on his little Sunfish sailboat followed by friend needing to be driven to the train to get back to the city immediately, condoms falling out of his pocket when he stuck out his hand to meet your friend's elderly mother at the gas station.

A few months later Mom decided to ditch the Upper East Side for Florida, which seemed like a gutsy divorced-lady-starting-over kind of move. My parents were physically farther apart than they had ever been. But there was some backpedaling after Mom was "asked" to leave the complex where she lived in the Sunshine State after only a few months, at which point she opted to crash in the West Village at my father's studio while she looked for her own place. My father had moved back to Manhattan from Amagansett after his relationship with a local woman named Pity ended, as one can imagine, badly. Reconvening in the West Village my parents now ate together, went to movies and checked each other in and out of the hospital. Some people might call this dating.

"Hi, baby. It's Mom. I'm at your father's."

Katharine and I had gotten an apartment in Brooklyn together after I graduated from Purchase. I scrounged through the ashtray looking for the roach Katharine had overlooked.

"I've left Florida," she said, pausing to let her line "land," as they say in the theater. The problem with my mother was that everything she said had a big landing. "I'm no longer on speaking terms with my hairdresser" went high into the air and came down at your feet with as much of a thud as "They've found a growth the size of a brioche under my left armpit."

"I've left Florida" sounded like she had left her Venezuelan dance teacher/lover and was now back with my father.

The last time I spoke with her, my mother said she was doing okay but that she missed minorities terribly.

"You left Florida because you miss black people?" I asked.

"Not just black people, Jeanne. Gays and Latinos and the Chinese and the Koreans."

"Lesbians?"

"Actually I've never thought lesbians add that much to the city, frankly. Anyway, I'm at your father's."

I sparked up the ashy doob I had gleaned. "Uh-huh."

"He's being absolutely impossible."

"Really?" I said in a loud, shocked way. My mother was the perfect "stone call," because she herself made no sense. People often make the mistake of trying to bring people to their level of sanity or sobriety or intelligence or what have you. A much more pleasurable option is to go to their special place for a few hours.

"I slept on a bed with no sheets last night. He said his sheets were at the Chinese place when I arrived. I said, 'Steve, do you mean to tell me you don't have any spare sheets?' The man doesn't have a set of spare sheets, dolly."

I puffed further on the doob, but it had gone out. I relit it.

"And he's sleeping on that rubber thing in the living room."

"The raft."

"The what?"

"The raft." Dad had a primitive inflatable mattress, extremely narrow, that looked like an actual raft you'd use at the beach. The air would go out of it as you slept so you woke up with a flat piece of rubber between you and the floor. He offered it up to relatives and friends who were in town.

"Stay at the Carlyle if you'd like, Hereford," he'd say, "but you're more than welcome to lay your head at my place during the trial. Very comfortable. Absolutely."

"Oh my God, it is a raft. The man is fifty-five years old and he's sleeping on a raft."

"On the banks of West Fourth Street. Sounds kinda Bob Dylany."

"Believe me, Bob Dylan has a nice suite up at the Waldorf. I guarantee you if you go to visit Bob Dylan there's sheets on the bed. Total insanity."

"Why don't you leave?"

"The man doesn't have two nickels to rub together. Did you

know your father sometimes sleeps upright, in his computer chair?"

"Why?"

"Apparently his asthma is so bad that he has to sleep upright sometimes to be able to breathe."

"Why doesn't he prop some pillows up in bed?"

"He's afraid he'll stop breathing if he lies flat in bed."

I hear my mother light a cigarette and exhale.

"Are you smoking in his house?"

"He's not here right now."

AFTER TWO DAYS of Mom staying with Dad, Eleanor calls from St. Vincent's Hospital.

"Hi. So Dad had a major asthma attack and . . . well, it's weird."

I hung up wondering what in the world Eleanor could mean by weird. Suspicious? Salacious? Depressing?

It was my birthday, so I had plans with my friends for later that night. But first I had to head to St. Vincent's third floor, down the corridor, through the double doors, past the nurse's station, on the right after the water fountain. I paused before opening the door to his room. I rolled my eyes, inhaled, exhaled, stared at the ceiling, chewed on the insides of my cheeks a little and started in the door. A nurse appeared.

"Who are you, dear?"

"I'm his daughter." I held up the pass I had gotten down-stairs for her to see. The six-by-four-inch plastic pass that read VISITOR was all she needed to verify my genetic honesty.

"Oh, okay, fine, dear. Now, you know your father had some reactions to the steroids?"

The nurse informed me that my father had gotten out of bed the previous night and hurled a wooden chair out the hospital window. The chair landed on Seventh Avenue, apparently killing no one.

"Wow."

"So I'm going to have to ask you not to give him anything he could possibly injure himself with."

Did she mean more chairs?

"He's been asking for a pen. And that could be dangerous. No pens."

I opened the door and went in. He wasn't in the first bed so I walked past the curtain to the second bed. His eyes opened the second I walked in, which disturbed me. I needed a minute to take the vision in. But I didn't get it.

His arms were tied with belts to the side of the bed, his legs were under belts as well. He had an oxygen mask on. He moved his head back and forth to wiggle it off his mouth so he could speak. It was like a gossipy corpse come back to life.

"Jean, thank God."

"Hi, Dad."

"Your timing is flawless as usual, Jean-Joe. Just flawless. Now, here's the plan."

I pulled up a chair.

"Now, have you got a pen on you?"

"Yes."

"Terrific. They won't be back for a while. Let me have that pen."

"I can't."

"They just gave me my medicine. The coast is clear."

"I can't give you a pen, Dad."

"What do you mean? Crazy talk. Give me the pen."

"The nurse said you might hurt yourself."

"Absolute nonsense. Jean, you can't imagine what's going on in the basement."

"I can't, Dad. I'm sorry."

My father looked at me from behind the eyes of insanity. He wanted to write down everything he'd seen. And I would not give him the means to do that. My father and I loved stories. And I was denying him this story—the story of his own insanity. Highly medicated, steroid-induced to be sure. But still, insanity.

"This place is an abortion mill, Jeanne. A Catholic hospital. With a goddamn abortion mill in the basement. I was invited to a party down there last night. A gal from the second floor asked if I'd like to go have a drink. A drink sounded all right after throwing that chair through the window, so I went. They've got these enormous black women serving drinks while abortions are being performed. I've got to get this down. That's just the beginning, Jean-Joe."

Just then my father wiggled his leg and his penis dribbled out of the covers. He didn't notice. He continued talking about the basement and the colored lights and the dancing. I pulled the blanket over him. My father is a Catholic but he's a liberal Democrat, pro-choice, so this party in the basement wasn't some psychedelic representation of his politics. I thought of my friends waiting for me at the restaurant. Carmen and my singer friend Sophia also had charming fathers who struggled to pay their rent and ruined your birthday and talked big. And loved you. Sometimes that was the worst part, seemingly more difficult than the deadbeat dads or the mean dads or the absentee workaholic dads—to have a father who was totally crazy pants who adored you was a special kind of agony.

I told my father once more that I couldn't give him a pen. He glared at me with his bulging blue eyes. He looked like all the pictures I had seen of his mother. She had the same bulging blue eyes. He had Crazy Kate eyes. The story about Crazy Kate's later years was that in the hospital toward the end of her life she saw bugs on the walls and demanded martinis from the nurses. He wriggled the oxygen mask back over his nose and mouth, took a few breaths, and then wriggled it off to speak. "I'll remember this, Jean. I'm going to remember this."

I walked out of the building and sat on the steps of the first brownstone and cried. I had no idea whether he would ever be normal again, if he ever was normal, if he was now a certifiable madman or if I was just a big fucking baby.

WHEN HIS BREATHING WAS regulated, the "dementia," which the hospital claimed was due to a bad reaction of a combination of drugs, went away. He left the hospital and went back to his little studio on the corner of Bank and West Fourth Street.

THE NEXT TIME I saw Dad was at the Corner Bistro for Eleanor's birthday. The Corner Bistro is known for its great cheeseburgers, crowded conviviality, and literary weirdos. It could also be one of the smokiest spots in Manhattan. It had served as my father's living room since he had moved to West Fourth Street. It had some appeal at first as a place you hung out with your divorced dad: it was lively and noisy and filled with cute young men and old characters, and its burgers were undeniably delicious. But it had its limitations. You couldn't get a table for a lot of people, a lot of the time you couldn't get a table at all, you were often sharing one with strangers, which is fun under normal circumstances, but when it's your birthday or some cousin is in town you don't really want old drunks ogling your *tetas* and breathing on your beer.

As I headed in I saw Eleanor and Mom at a table in the bar with some strangers, Katharine and Dad were standing just to the right of the table with beers in their hands, talking. Julia was sitting at the bar, talking to the bartender. I went over and gave Dad a kiss hello and leaned over the table and kissed Mom on the cheek.

"Here she is, ladies and gentlemen of the jury, the turncoat of Fourteenth Street. Don't think for one second, my dear, that I've forgotten the absolute treachery that took place at St. Vincent's." He laughed and patted me on the back.

"Dad, that nurse specifically told me not to give you a pen."

"Because they sure as hell knew I was going to take down their whole basement operation with it. What'll you have? Beer?"

I nodded.

"Steve," Mom chimed in, "you were like a wild beast in there. I don't think you get it."

"You could have killed someone with that chair, Dad," Eleanor said.

"Killed someone? Eleanor, I would have enjoyed it. Oh, I was really out of it."

Julia came over to the table and said in my ear, "That bartender is a total asshole."

I looked over. I couldn't tell if he was an asshole, but he was oldish and had a big butt.

"Why is he an asshole?"

"Because we're talking and laughing and having a great time and I ask if he wants my number and he says, 'I'm afraid I've got myself a girlfriend, love.'"

"And?"

"You don't say that to a woman, Jeanne."

"Why not?"

Dad came over and handed me my beer. I wondered if he had poisoned it, considering how mad he was about the fuckin' pen.

"Because it's rude."

"It's the truth."

Julia laughed. "Okay, true. Let's move on, shall we?"

Sipping my beer, I thought about a cigarette, but the place was so fucking smoky already it was killing my potential smoke. It was like trying to be a writer with Dad around, trying to booze it up with Mom around. I wanted to live the poor artist's life in the West Village, I wanted to drink like a maniac, but Mom and Dad had "smoked up the room" already, they were hogging all the death and destruction for themselves, making it hard for me to enjoy destroying myself.

Dad was less than a week out of the St. Vincent's abortion mill, the proverbial hospital "woods," and now I could barely make out his features a mere two feet away from me because of the cigarette haze. I could hear him through it, though, and he was having a grand time, smoke or no smoke.

AFTER MORE BEERS and some burgers, Dad suggested we all move on to his place and have some birthday cake. We made our way down the block to his building and headed up the narrow staircase to his apartment. Dad's apartment, which was never locked, was on the second floor of a charming nineteenth-century red-brick three-story building. There was the owner's apartment on the first floor, two apartments on the second floor and one on the top floor. Dad's upstairs neighbors, a pretty Asian woman and her photographer boyfriend, passed us on the stairs.

"Mei Ling, Richard, these are my daughters: Julia, Jeanne, Katharine and Eleanor, who's twenty-six today. Will you join us for a glass of wine and a piece of birthday cake?"

Julia glared at me. "Jesus Christ, does he have to?"

I left Dad, Mei Ling and Richard in the hall and went inside. Dad simply had no concept that his apartment might not be the Hyannis Port of the West Village; he would invite way more people over to this place than could possibly fit or than he could properly entertain. You entered Dad's and were in the kitchen. The kitchen was a very narrow counter that began at the front door and ran about three feet into the apartment. There were a couple cheapo cabinets above the counter. There was a tiny sink and a half-fridge under the counter. A toaster and a dish rack and the old pasta maker from our house in Bronxville took up all the counter space. This part of the apartment felt like Gregor Samsa's Winnebago. When Dad cooked (opening jars of olives, frying chicken eyeballs), there was a leaf that came up. The drawers in the kitchen held everything from odds-and-ends silverware, pens, letter openers and loose change to a meat thermometer from the early '70s and an electric knife. Opposite the kitchen was the bathroom with its accordion door made of plywood.

The main room was approximately twelve feet by twelve feet. There were two windows facing West Fourth Street. Dad claimed there were two young Swedes who cleaned the apartment directly across the street in the nude once a week. Dad's long desk was the main piece of furniture, with his big PC and printer and scanner and gargantuan *Oxford English Dictionary*.

The brown metal fluorescent lamp had seemed cool when I was little but looked depressing now. Ditto for all the gray metal file cabinets. There was a futon couch/bed that never made it to couch mode, it was permanently reclined. There was a skinny spiral staircase that once led to the apartment upstairs but now was blocked off. Next to the vestigial staircase lay the raft, shriveled in a clump. The second room was a tiny space with a drafty window. Most people would have designated this the bedroom and cordoned it off with some decorative touch, like a door, but Dad just filled it with random boxes of books.

Mom opened the accordion door of the bathroom and came out right as I was entering the apartment and there was an awkward "You go," "No, after you" moment. We all gathered the best we could in a space that had one chair and a reclined futon. Mom took the big swivel office chair and Eleanor enlisted Katharine to help her fold the futon into a couch. Julia scooched onto the chair with Mom, who was teeny enough to allow it, and I scooched onto the futon with Eleanor and Katharine despite their identical *Fuck off* looks.

Dad eventually moseyed in from the hall. "Aren't those two terrific?"

"Dad, do you have to invite everyone you see to things?" Julia said.

"They're not everyone, they're my neighbors. He did some terrific work a few years back photographing Chernobyl, a ghoulish assignment if ever there was one." Dad went into the kitchen and opened the mini-fridge, calling back to his daughters and ex-wife, "And she's a knockout, isn't she?"

He took Eleanor's birthday cake out of the mini-fridge and brought it into the living room.

"Now, this place is terrific. The best," he said, putting the cake on the desk.

Claude's *was* the best. And expensive. Which is why we were a little shocked.

"Steve, how about a cake knife?" Mom said, trying to help things along.

"A what?"

"A cake knife? And some plates?"

"Absolutely. Absolutely." Dad headed back into the kitchen, where he rummaged around. "Jean-Joe, why don't you put *La Traviata* on the hi-fi? It should be right there."

Eleanor let out a little huff. She hated opera, drunkenness, Dad, Mom and the West Village. Dad came back into the room with a knife and three plates for six people. He handed the knife to Eleanor.

"Eleanor-a, birthday girl, why don't you do the honors?"

"What kind is it, Dad?" Katharine asked.

"Chocolate ganache, I believe."

Everyone watched Eleanor open the white box.

"Dad!" Eleanor screamed. "There's a piece missing!"

"Oh, for God's sake, Steve." Mom gasped.

"It was half-price with a piece missing. We don't need that piece! To hell with that piece!"

Mom got up. "I'm going outside for a cigarette."

Eleanor remained speechless, looking at the fancy cake with a piece missing.

I got up to see if I could put together a team of forks. Six forks—well, five, seeing as Mom wasn't going to be eating—was going to be a nice challenge. I found three forks and a plastic spoon and some chopsticks.

"Jean, what happened to *La Traviata*?"

I stepped over a box of files and put on the record. I tasted the cake and looked at Eleanor angrily stabbing her cake. It was delicious. Dad asked if anyone wanted some wine, Julia went down to have a cigarette with Mom, and Eleanor looked at her watch, waiting until enough time had passed and she could head back uptown to her apartment to watch TV.

Dad gave me some red wine and said, "At least she went to the stoop to smoke. Normally she just smokes up here and blows it out the window but it still comes in. I can't tell you how that smoke is affecting me."

"Considering you just nearly died from an asthma attack, is it really such a hot idea for her to smoke in your apartment?" I asked.

"I hadn't thought of that. You might have a point."

I headed downstairs and mooched a True Blue from Mom.

"Honestly." She took a puff and watched a large gay man move past us with his Lhasa apso. "A birthday cake with a piece missing? I could kill him."

"Or you could stay somewhere else . . ." I offered up.

"Yeah, Mom, you don't have to put up with his shit. Men are ridiculous," Julia said.

"Right, and, well, you don't have to put up with anything you don't want to because you are, in fact, no longer married,"

I said, trying once more to convey the basic concept of divorce to these two, who seemed not to understand that a significant part of divorce entailed not seeing each other. They were like slaves who didn't know where to go once they had been set free.

"The man bought a cake with a piece missing for his daughter's birthday, Jeanne. Now, I ask you, is that normal?"

"No, Mom, it's not but the thing is . . . you don't have to eat the cake or look at the cake or anything. Unlike the four of us, you can just walk away."

"It just irritates the hell out of me is all."

And then my mother revealed that she had signed a lease on an apartment on Greenwich Street a few weeks earlier. She could have moved into her own apartment weeks before Eleanor's birthday, weeks before she put Dad in the emergency room at St. Vincent's.

"I can't possibly stay here one more minute." She lit a new cigarette and exhaled defensively. "I'm not married to the man, you know."

"That's what I've been trying to say."

I squished my cigarette on the step and looked out at West Fourth Street. The guy who owned the bookstore across the street was throwing some boxes onto the curb. It was past ten and he was still open. The place was totally disorganized and dusty and small. It had no regular hours. The neighborhood had so many guys like this one. People who seemed like they had fascinating lives, a lot whose best moments seemed behind them. Gays whose '70s were over, models whose Hep C was what remained from the '80s, elderly actors who spent their days on the phone with Equity, trying to get a little assistance.

Once my mother was finally settled in her new apartment she and my father still liked to hang around the neighborhood together, go to the Biography Bookshop, people-watch on his stoop.

"YOUR MOTHER AND I have a failed divorce," my father said to me over greasy eggs a few days later at La Bonbonniere on Eighth Avenue. "We gave it our best shot. We really did. It just didn't work out." The waitress, a character-actress brunette in her early thirties, parked her cigarette in an ashtray and came over and filled our cheap porcelain coffee cups with more coffee.

"My God, what timing! Terrific. Thank you very much," Dad said to the waitress.

As she walked away he leaned in ever so slightly and said, "Now, there's a stunner, huh?"

I AM NOT AN IDIOTE!

I HAVE BAD JUDGMENT, or no judgment. Like Lenny in *Of Mice and Men,* I pet things too hard and then hide the evidence. Around the time my parents were dating in the West Village, Katharine and I got an apartment together in Brooklyn and I got my first post-college job. I was temping at a law firm, a white-shoe law firm. (I have no idea why people still use this expression—it should just be called a white-people law firm.) A group of about twenty of us "coders" sat in a large room, jacked up on terrible free coffee, coding documents. "Coding" meant that we marked documents containing any mention of this one particular case. It was really just high-level word jumbles. "I see the plaintiff from the case's name, okay, circle that, move on to next document." I got fired because after about four months the firm calculated that I was finishing something like 1.2 docs an hour when most people were doing somewhere around two hundred. My new work friend Kristina was fired, too. We both lived in Brooklyn and had no idea what we were going to do for work. Nineteen ninety was a shitty time to be out of work and skill-free. I had

also been fired from my second job as a "trainer" at the New
York Sports Club around the corner from my house. I had
no knowledge of physiology or exercise or sports medicine,
but they gave me a special shirt and called me a trainer. On
my dinner break I'd walk the two blocks to my house and
smoke a couple cigarettes and go back to work. I was fired for
smelling like smoke even though I denied being a smoker and
blamed it on my sister Katharine, who did not smoke. "It's terrible," I told my boss. "We share a closet and my clothes end
up smelling like smoke. Disgusting." She didn't buy it.

KRISTINA AND I WORKED briefly for NYPIRG (New York
Public Interest Research Group), canvassing Park Slope on
environmental issues. We would knock on a few doors in
the November cold and then, despite being paid on commission, decide to hide out at her house, where she would make
her Tuna Peewiggle (fusilli pasta, capers, tuna and olive oil)
and we'd smoke a billion cigarettes and talk about how much
NYPIRG sucked and what we really should be doing. Kristina
had studied filmmaking at NYU briefly, before dropping out
because of some kind of pressure to live up to the work of her
great-uncle, Surrealist filmmaker Luis Buñuel.

"I would stand on the corner of University and Tenth trying
to set up a shot with other students and my teachers would stop
by to watch what I was doing. Luis is obviously this legendary
figure at the film school. I, uh, what do they say in baseball?"

Kristina started to giggle and her eyes were tearing up. I start laughing maniacally also.

"Choked. I choked."

"You'll get it back," I said.

"No, I won't. I'm a half-artist. I'm smart and talented but I'm not tough enough to go the distance. It's a curse being a half-artist, caught between being a normal person and a real creative person. I'm nuts like a good artist, but I don't have anything to show for it."

I wasn't exactly going the distance with anything. Carmen and I smoked a lot of pot and talked about doing another two-woman show. I was a quarter-artist at best.

KRISTINA AND I GOT the idea to start a housecleaning business together, one with some pizzazz. Around this time, Leona Helmsley was sentenced to jail for tax evasion and Zsa Zsa Gabor had been sent to the slammer for slapping a cop. So Kristina and I decided to call our new business "Leona and Zsa Zsa's Big House Cleaning Service," and we made a flyer with images of diamond baubles, tiaras and prison pantsuits. We lasted for two houses—a giant old cluttered dungeon of a brownstone in Park Slope and a pity job on Thirty-first Street from Kristina's friend—before we realized we weren't cut out for housework. It was back to regular jobs for us. During all this, Kristina and I had become good friends.

Our luck turned when I landed a job as an office manager

for a company that made signs where I could wear my running shorts to work. Kristina, even less fashiony than I, got a job as the secretary to the editor of *Harper's Bazaar*, Anthony Mazzola.

One day we were on the phone at our new jobs and Kristina mentioned that she had spent the morning opening RSVPs to some big gala Mr. Mazzola was throwing and that she had just left a message for Lauren Hutton asking whether she would be attending.

"Kristina, I gotta go. I'm getting a fax."

A handwritten fax from my boss (sitting four feet away in his office) came through, addressed to me and his wife, Lois, who was the chief financial officer of the company. It read: YOU TWO ARE GOING TO BE LOOKING FOR WORK SOON IF YOU DON'T GET OFF YOUR ASSES AND START DOING THINGS MY WAY, THE HIGH WAY, THE RIGHT WAY, THE ONLY WAY. SHAPE UP, MORONS.—YOUR BOSS.

Marty sent out these threatening faxes a couple times a week, but I thought it was strange that he included his wife. Couldn't he yell at her in private, apart from the twenty-two-year-old in jogging shorts who ordered pencils for the office? Marty was the kind of guy who was always on a Slim-Fast diet but couldn't grasp the idea that you don't drink a Slim-Fast and then eat a big lunch. That it's one or the other.

I went to the supply room and tried to find something to do that would get Marty off my case, something that would prove to him that I, at least, was not a moron. In the supply room I ran into Margo, a graphic designer who lived in the East Village and was slumming it at this sign company. We decided it was time for a mid-morning cigarette, so we went back to her desk. All the production managers and graphic designers had tilted drawing desks with ashtrays on them.

After the cig I headed back to my desk and decided to prank-call Kristina.

"*Harper's Bazaar.* Anthony Mazzola's office," Kristina answered coolly.

In a breathy, super-deep voice, I said, "Is Anthony in?"

"No, he's not. Who's calling, please?" she said in her stiff office voice that let me know she didn't know it was me. Jackpot.

"It's Lauren. Hutton."

"Oh! Hello, Miss Hutton. My name is Kristina. Anthony and Michele are out to lunch."

"Well, then, I suppose that leaves us a little time to get to know each other."

"Oh, uh . . ." Kristina stumbled uncomfortably. My God, she was an easy target!

"You're new, I suppose? Because I haven't heard a thing about you."

"Yes, that's right. I'm brand-new."

"I like new," I purred.

"Being new is awkward, yes, well, for me it is."

"I'll help you, dear." I cackled a little.

Kristina laughed nervously.

"First thing we'll do is spread your legs and I'll lick that beautiful pussy of yours," I said, stifling a laugh.

"Oh my goodness, Miss Hutton, I, I . . . I think you're trying to shock me, I, I . . ." Kristina was remarkably polite and, well, adorable.

"Now, what time is that party again? Oh, this will be a lot more fun than I thought . . ." I said.

"Eight o'clock, I, um," she sputtered, and ran out of etiquette.

"Tell Anthony I can't wait to see him and I really can't wait to see you . . . Kristina."

I hung up and almost fell off my cheapo office chair in my little cubicle. I'd been prank-calling people for years, this is just the kind of simple pleasure I never tire of, but Kristina was a level of gullible I hadn't encountered. Wow, that was fun, I thought to myself. I can't figure out why nobody ever hires me for an acting job.

Marty came up and leaned on the carpeted wall that was my cubicle divider.

"Uh, Miss Office Manager–slash–Carwash Worker—you look like something out of that movie *Car Wash*, you remember that movie? Follow me, I want to go over some things with you and that other numbskull."

"Lois went to get lunch."

"Okay, then make me a Slim-Fast shake quick and meet me in my office. And don't tell Lois I had a shake when she comes back."

About two hours later I made it back to my desk alive from my meeting with Marty. There were no messages from Kristina, so I guessed she hadn't figured out that I was the genius who'd pranked her. I grabbed the phone and dialed her.

"Good afternoon, *Harper's Bazaar*. Anthony Mazzola's office."

"Hey. It's me."

"Oh my God. Hi."

"Hi. What's up?"

"Holy Fucking Shit is what's up. You're not going to believe this," she said.

Try me, I thought to myself.

"Lauren Hutton called earlier today to RSVP to Anthony's gala . . ."

"Yeah." I was now giggling quietly.

"And she said the most disgusting thing to me, Jeanne."

"She did? What?" I asked, looking around the office to make sure nobody was going to interrupt the fun.

"She said she wanted to eat my pussy at the gala!"

"She SAID that? Are you sure she wasn't just being nice 'cause you're new and everything?"

"JEANNE! She said, 'I want to spread your legs and lick that beautiful pussy of yours!'"

"Lauren Hutton said that?"

"Yes!" Kristina was yelling now.

"Holy fucking shit," I said. This was the best ever.

"Yeah. So I told Anthony what happened," Kristina said.

"You WHAT?" I yelled.

"I told Anthony what she said. I went into his office when they got back from lunch and told Anthony and Michele the whole thing. They're livid."

"What the fuck did you do THAT for?"

"Well, what was I supposed to do? Let Lauren Hutton go down on me just because we're in a recession?"

"But, but—"

"Jeanne! It's the principle! You can't let people talk to you like that just because you're a secretary!" Kristina had a lot of principles.

"They're going to call her and confront her in a minute, so I can't talk long."

"They're what? Oh my God," I said. "Fuck, Kristina." She was my new friend. We were having so much fun. "That was me."

"What was you?"

"On the phone."

"What are you talking about?"

"That was me pretending to be Lauren Hutton." I was the worst person in New York.

"What? That was you? Jeanne! What the fuck is wrong with you?"

I flashed to my childhood insistence: "I am not an ID-I-OTE! Do not call me one!"

"I thought it would be . . . funny," I said.

"Funny? You thought it would be funny? I just told my boss that Lauren Hutton said she wanted to eat my pussy! Do you have any idea how uncomfortable that was? Mr. Mazzola is in his sixties! God. Now I have to go in there and tell him and his wife that it was my friend, my friend who called pretending to be Lauren Hutton wanting to eat my pussy."

"I'm so sorry."

"Jesus Christ, Jeanne. Why didn't you tell me it was you?"

"I was going to call you right back but then Marty came over and made me do a bunch of stuff. I . . . I meant to call you right back. I didn't think, I mean I never thought you'd tell your boss about it."

"I was really upset! Really upset! Jesus Christ, I told Anthony I'd been sexually harassed, those words, 'sexually harassed' by Lauren Hutton!"

"Oh, boy."

"Yeah. Oh, boy. I gotta go. I gotta go make sure they don't call her and yell at her. They're definitely going to fire me."

My friend was now about to be back out there, eating Tuna Peewiggle every night, looking for work in a terrible economy. All thanks to my unparalleled sense of humor.

They didn't fire her, but she must have felt like a total asshole for the rest of the time she worked for him. As in, Yes, here I am typing a letter for you, longtime esteemed editor-in-chief of *Harper's Bazaar*, and here I am wearing appropriate office wear, but when I leave here I'm going to go hang out with my super-sophisticated friends—people who prank-call their friends at work pretending to be celebrities in search of some office carpet.

I, however, did get fired. A few weeks after the Lauren Hutton incident, Marty told me as he was leaving the office that some air-conditioning guys were coming to fix the AC downstairs in the large workshop.

"Don't let those motherfuckers downstairs alone! They'll fuck me so hard!"

I didn't have a chance to ask Marty why they weren't allowed downstairs, why they would fuck him so hard. I assumed he thought they were going to steal from him—tools from the workshop perhaps. The guy was wasted on Slim-Fast, rushing around and yelling at everyone. Everybody was out to fuck him and always quite hard.

When the AC guys came I was playing cards with Margo and smoking cigs, learning about her fascinating older-lady sex life. I buzzed them in and told them which AC was broken, letting them go downstairs to work on it while I hung with Margo.

Marty came back from his meeting early and walked up to my desk, where I was ordering paper for the fax machine.

"The AC guys are finished?" he barked.

"No, they're still working," I said, smiling.

"You fucking crazy woman! You're trying to kill me, too?" He ran at full speed in his suit to the stairs and I followed. "I told you not to leave them here alone!"

We reached the lower floor, where the guys were working on the big unit, and Marty turned to me and yelled, "You're trying to kill me!" He picked up an eight-foot-long piece of metal tubing and swung it around his head repeatedly, lasso style.

"I forgot! I forgot!" I said, ducking and weaving away from the metal pipe.

Marty never apologized for trying to decapitate me with a lead pipe. He suspended me and Lois for a week for "moronic behavior during work hours," and the first day of my suspension he called me and fired me.

I'M LAZY. I'm forgetful. I go too far. I don't know when to stop. I need to grow up. I am not a people person, nor am I organized or highly organized, enthusiastic or responsible. I'm not a self-starter or a problem solver. I don't have good phone or computer skills. I can't multitask or work well with others. And yet I maintain: I am not an id-i-ote.

ELAINE MAYBE

CARMEN, my best friend and writing/performing partner had joined this theater company that went to Maine for two weeks every August to work out ideas for the upcoming season. Being a native New Yorker and not someone that familiar with the woods or white people and definitely not the combination, Carmen asked if she could bring me along. I saw this as a free Maine vacation, the summer tennis camp I never had, and gladly went. I wasn't doing much, just waitressing at this place on Montague Street called The Leaf and Bean. I don't know if I could be described as a "good" waitress. Eleanor and her husband came in for brunch one day and there was a long line and a couple came and stood behind them and she heard the guy say, "Well, I don't know. Why don't you go check?" and the woman walked to the front of the café and then came back and said to her boyfriend, "Yeah, she's working today," and they walked out. I had a certain style. Either you got it or you didn't.

Almost before I stepped out of the car I met this actor named Jed and became a company member of the Irondale

Ensemble Project. Back in New York, I began doing the out-reach work of the company, part of which was teaching acting in high schools in the Bronx and way out in Brooklyn. I also commenced being the girlfriend of the young, handsome, funny, rich, charming, talented Mr. Jed Clarke.

The guy was about as nice as they come. Nicer. Always the first one to show up for a cleanup day at his building or offer his Westphalia van to someone who needed to move. The kind of no-fuss guy who shopped for khakis at EMS on Broadway even though he was retail royalty, his great-grandfather having started the swankiest clothing store in New York. The way he saw it, EMS was around the corner, easier than going above Fourteenth Street. People who do things because they're easy drive me nuts! Hard! Hard is what you want! That's what makes it mean something. That's what makes it real, dummy! His attitude toward my writing was similarly oppressive.

"I think you should do whatever makes you happy. You're an amazing writer. You should go for it."

Go for it. Go-for-it. I was doomed. My writing . . . doomed.

Jed's conversation was packed with clichés. Some of his most oft-used were: now you're cooking with gas, let's get down to brass tacks, and there's more than one way to skin a cat. Jed would drop them casually and I'd think, What are you doing? Jesus, keep it down, looking around to make sure no one had heard him. He was a big reader but he read so goddamn freely. This looks good. My brother gave me this, I'll read this next. No thought about what he should be reading. He just read.

Part of my life was cohesive: waitress, member of a serious downtown theater company with a social conscience that taught AIDS education in prisons, schools, homeless shelters. We performed Brecht and Büchner. And then there was my after-work life, which involved a big loft in SoHo and fundraisers with his parents and dinner at '21.'

Jed and I got our food from Dean & Deluca. Deep down I knew Dean & Deluca was not a grocery store. We watched TV on his big screen. This was terrifying to me. His couch was big and comfortable. Comfort? I'll never be a writer. He had cable. Cable! Not one word will I write. He wanted to get married. He wanted kids. I loved him a lot. We laughed constantly. But just what kind of life was this guy setting me up for? I would go to the corner every day and buy the *New York Times* and read it with my coffee. By that time Jed had flipped on his big TV and was watching CNN. I'd try to block out the headline scroll, the dramatic language, the graphic photography but you can't. TV is TV—it can't be blocked out. It's TV. Clenching the paper every morning I'd think, I'm trying to do something here! It's TBA, but still.

I was terrified that if I stayed with Jed I would lose something I wasn't even sure I had. Focus? Drive? Talent? I can't concentrate if it's just gonna be fine and dandy around here all the time. How can anyone think in all this peace and comfort?

I moved in with Jed and got a waitressing gig in Manhattan at a café called Le Gamin on Twenty-first and Ninth, and at the one in SoHo. The owners, Robert and Hervé, were completely bonkers, partiers, fun, super-French—they always took the staff's side against a customer. "Get ze ell out of ear. We doan need your bullshit, lady!" They were awesome. I liked to think waitressing at a French place had more, I don't know what—*je ne sais quoi?*—than other restaurants. Besides the French owners, there was a cook from Mali and his wife who spoke no English, and many of our regulars were French. People speaking French around me made it less like regular old waitressing. I could be myself there because I felt like everyone who worked there was unhappy and had a good time being that way. Unlike an office atmosphere, where I felt I couldn't wear something as daring as a bright orange cardigan—ooooh, bright!—at Le Gamin during a heat wave I waitressed in my vintage Betty Grable green bathing suit. The owners seemed to hire people because they were wild and funny and didn't take any bullshit.

Katharine called me one day and asked if I wanted to be on this late-night TV show she was producing called *Last Call*. There had been a law passed that it was now legal to be top-less in New York State parks, beaches and the subway sys-tem. The woman heading up this change called it the top-free movement. The producers of *Last Call* wanted to do a seg-ment on it and were sitting around trying to figure out who they could get, a normal person, someone who wasn't in the sex industry, to ride the subway topless.

"My sister will do it," Katharine said.

"How much?" I said when she called me.

"A hundred and fifty."

"What? A hundred and fifty. No way. Five hundred."

"Jean, I've got to do this segment as cheaply as possible."

"You're my sister. Aren't you supposed to be pimping me out for the most money possible?"

"I'm also the producer here, Jeanne. Two hundred."

"Four hundred."

"Three hundred. Final offer."

"Done. Oh, I want a bodyguard." Not that my boobs were going to cause anyone to go insane, but boobs are boobs, you never know.

"Fine. One bodyguard."

I met my sister and the film crew at the uptown E train at Fiftieth Street. A svelte brunet man ran up to me and waved a small lead pipe in front of my face like a sparkler.

"Hi! I'm Craig! I'm your bodyguard!" and he did a little fancy dance step right there on the platform. I felt so safe. Katharine walked over.

"Hi!"

"Katharine—"

Craig was dancing and jabbing his pipe into the air. Rehearsing. Katharine turned to me.

"Okay, look, I called some bodyguards. No one was available. Craig is awesome. He's danced for some really good companies."

"Brother. Fine."

The shoot went off without too much trouble. We had to duck the New York City police as we didn't have permits, and we couldn't film on a train with kids or a train that was too full. But it went fine.

Jed wasn't too eager for his family to hear about my she-nanigans, particularly his grandmother. Jed's family was so out of the regular work world that his mother, Diane, thought it was adorable that I was a waitress and said to me one day, excitedly, "So do you say, 'Hi, my name is Jeanne and I'll be your waitress?'"

These were people who didn't even ride the subway, let alone without clothes on national television. While Jed's family lived on Fifth, my parents were living in filth.

One day Dad was going for a run in his neighborhood in his grungy running uniform: holey T-shirt, jogging shorts à la 1971, red-white-and-blue sweatbands on his wrists and also around his head. He was on his corner waiting to cross the street and begin his run when a homeless guy at his side said to him, "It's murder out there today."

And my dad said, "What do you mean?"

"People don't want to give anything at all. You getting much today?"

My dad realized the guy thought he was a fellow home-less panhandler. My father thought it was funny but the story was met with some silence from my sisters and me when he told it. It was just too close. It's one thing if some rich person thinks you're homeless but when a seasoned pro thinks you're one of them that's another thing.

My father blew through the house money in approximately two years. When you're fifty-five years old with no job, no retirement money, no pension, you'd think you might want to at least buy a little apartment in Montclair, New Jersey, or somewhere, to live in. But he was going to hit it big with Stylebook. And now it was a nonfiction book on Fitzgerald. He was now taking temp work, borrowing a few bucks here and there. He borrowed twenty bucks from Katharine when she was a brand-new peon at a publishing house making around $12,000 a year, and after she gave it to him she got up in the middle of the restaurant and screamed, "You are the worst father ever! I hate you!" and walked out.

As for my mother, she didn't look homeless, but she was becoming less and less of a mother you could take out in public. She had a uniform: a black pencil skirt, gray cashmere cowl neck, long pearls which always got hooked on one breast, black stockings, stylish black heels (high), lit cigarette, jangly charm bracelets of her mother's, and gold bangles and gold and platinum rings. She would no sooner wear silver than she would a candy necklace. This was what she wore when she went out, except sometimes she lost part of her outfit.

That summer Kate had a bunch of friends get married. By the fall, she needed to buy some wedding gifts and she wanted to hit the boutiques along Bleecker Street. She called Mom and they decided on lunch at Tartine and then some shopping. Mom was wearing her usual outfit. After lunch they hit a slew of stores up and down Bleecker. Coming out of Pierre Deux, Mom shrieked, "Oooh! Where's my skirt?"

Kate looked down and Mom was indeed missing her standard size-one black pencil skirt that she had been wearing earlier in the day. The rest of her uniform was intact: poof of faux-blond soufflé balanced on top of a gray cowl neck, long strand of pearls, black opaque stockings showcasing a pair of gams that would have made Ann Miller get a desk job, black undies underneath the stockings, and three-and-a-half-inch Joan & David black pumps.

"Mom!" Kate yelled, totally startled and baffled. "Where's your skirt?"

"I don't know, Kate. It was here a minute ago. Oh, for God's sake." Mom lit a cigarette to calm herself and focus on the case of the missing skirt.

"Were you wearing it when we left the restaurant?" Kate asked, panicked, looking through her bag for something to tie around Mom's torso.

"I must have been, don't you think?" Mom asked, less concerned about her current state of undress than intrigued by the puzzle of it all, as if it were just another trick Will Shortz had up his sleeve for her. Two young women walked by Kate and Mom, locking eyes on Mom's stockinged rear.

"Jesus, Mom. Should we get a cab?" Kate said.

"Are you out of your mind? That's a brand-new Calvin Klein skirt!"

Kate began huffing loudly. "Well (huff), I don't (huff-huff), Jesus, Mom (huff), I mean, Jesus."

"I went to the bathroom at Tartine and I'm pretty damn sure I had it on when I came out." Mom parked her cigarette between her lips and began running her hands up and down her sides and under her sweater. She felt something in her sweater and pulled it downward and out popped one black Calvin Klein skirt. "Oh, for heaven's sake!" Mom said, cackling with delight. "Here it is, Kate!"

Kate cackled, too, as Mom pulled it over her hips and smoothed it down with her hand.

"I'd hate to think how many stores we were in since lunch," Mom laughed.

"Yeah, I sorta thought of that."

"Let's go have a beer at the White Horse."

I took care of her Jack Russell, Emma, one weekend when she was in the hospital for one of her ailments. (She had surgery on both hands for carpal tunnel syndrome, which she believed she got from horseback riding; she had sciatica, a shooting pain that began at the base of her spine and ran down both legs—a horrific pain that she said was relieved best by a drink; and something called spinal stenosis. She always had a headache and could take four aspirin without water, crunching them up in her teeth like they were pistachios; she had high blood pressure; she had shingles; she had an ulcer that Eleanor claims is when Mom's interest in salt, coffee and spicy foods really took off. As for her beautiful blue eyes, she never let you forget one had a scratched cornea and one had a detached retina and she was legally blind. She also had "obtuse-angle" glaucoma, but she didn't need to smoke pot for it or anything, just to mention it whenever there was a break in the conversation. She was deaf in her right ear, she had depression, obviously, and took antidepressants.) Out on a walk, Emma pooped out a bunch of True Blue cigarette filters. When I told my mother about this, she just said, "Oh, that Emma. She just gets into everything." Mom wouldn't acknowledge the dirty, depressing mess in her apartment, her cigarette-pooping dog or her drinking. Her dog walker talked to my mom and took Emma home with him for good one day. I think we all wished he could have taken Mom home with him, too.

Jed's family was normal compared with Mom and Dad. Then again, most people were normal compared with Mom and Dad.

Jed was also sober, which was adorable and exotic.

"He's a junkie," I proudly described my new boyfriend to my friends.

"*Was* a junkie. He's been sober for a year. He quit dope at the Chelsea Hotel, where he was living." I'd really never known anyone who did drugs. When I told my parents about him, they just couldn't put it all together.

"His parents live on Fifth and Ninety-third and he was a junkie, you say? That can't be right," my mother said.

"He's sober now," I said, but they had no idea what that meant. "We're all sober, honey, until we start drinking" was their understanding of it. I barely knew what it meant myself, because my mom had never gotten any sober time outside of a rehab.

Mom loved to emphasize the fact that he was a junkie, I suppose, because it made her feel better about her own drinking.

Drugs were really bad, she implied, as she sat in her crummy West Village place, chain-smoking and drunk most of the time now. At this point she was forbidden to drink at any family events—no one would be around her if she was drinking—so she began transporting vodka in her big bottle of contact lens solution, which Dad squirted in his eye one day: "God damn it, Doris, what the hell is in here?" But drugs? "We don't do drugs, sweet pea. We're from Ladue."

Jed's sobriety never even registered with my dad. My dad registered Jew even though Jed was about a quarter Jewish, Jewish-ish, and had never practiced Judaism. They both liked Jed a lot, everyone liked him. But where my mom saw junkie my dad saw Jew and after giving me a book of poetry by Ezra Pound became concerned, chronically concerned, that Jed might consider having Pound's work around an insult.

"I hope to hell I haven't offended Jed with that book of Pound I gave you. Just love him up to World War Two, before he began the anti-Semitic radio addresses and all that. I'm not saying anything good about Pound after World War Two, but before the war, my God. Give it a try. Is the Pound going to be a problem for Jed?"

Jed, like many people, would have no idea that the poet Ezra Pound was the Mel Gibson of his day, nor would Jed even identify as a Jew.

"No, Dad. It's fine."

Jed and I were on a Somerset Maugham kick, working our way through everything he wrote, his short stories (*Rain*), his novels, *Of Human Bondage* and *The Razor's Edge*. My father thought he was a total waste of time. "You might want to try Proust again, Jean-Joe. I know you struggled the first time around. Give it another try." Or what? I always wanted to say. I liked *Swann's Way*. I did. I just pooped out. Jed took me to Paris and I brought it with me, that's how honorable my intentions were, that's what an incredibly well-intentioned kind of reader I am. I was going to read it on my first trip to Europe as I ate madeleines and shit. I like Proust. I honestly do, I just got sidetracked. Distractée.

Jed being sober and me not being sober was, at first, our act. He's sober. She's a big ol' boozehound! They're Jed and Jeanne, the yin-yang, sober-sloshed couple of the year!

I QUIT IRONDALE, the theater company Jed and I were members of. Eliot, the artistic director had cast me as a baguette in the latest production, *Danton's Death*, and I called him up at home one night, demanding to know what his problem was.

"Jeanne, I'm sorry if you're upset. I know crowd scenes aren't the most challenging. I'm sure you'd like to do more but at this point I don't feel you're ready to speak onstage."

Not ready to speak onstage. I was twenty-five. Under Eliot's tutelage I would be speaking onstage by what, thirty? Perhaps speaking and walking and holding my head up by forty-two? While I knew he was some kind of grant-writing, socially responsible woman-hater, I was also becoming aware that acting was a profession that would be filled with a-holes making all the decisions. Casting people. I had an agent but I wasn't tearing it up in the world of auditions. When I would go in for auditions I never showed my ass or body because I'm . . . stupid? Years later I would read that when she was starting out, Francis McDormand, the coolest actress ever, would wear what she called "cutlets" on auditions. Things she stuck in her bra to make it appear she had breasts. I never booked anything. Maybe I was stupid or maybe I sucked. Maybe I really sucked.

After I quit Irondale, I went to a theater school on Forty-second Street, where I wrote a play. This play went over big. Randy, the director of the school, came up to me afterward and said, "Jeanne, this play was awful. I expected something great from you. What happened?"

There seemed to be such an easy answer to the question Could I write? Could I write plays and stories and be some kind of nonacting actor or performer? Could I be the next Elaine May? Could I do weird things like the performance artists I studied in college but perhaps not be so unfunny? The answer was: why bother? You've got this awesome, funny guy you love, he's rich, life is easy, you're good friends. Do this. Don't do what you don't know. You might fail. You might be alone. You'll definitely be broke. It seemed like an either/or proposition. I had no idea that people could be ambitious and happy, financially stable and creative, content and interesting, domestic and nonsuicidal.

Around year three of our relationship, Jed's sobriety began to wear on my nerves. And he began complaining about my drinking.

"You become a different person when you drink," he'd say, pointing out what to me had always seemed like one of the benefits of drinking. He had a name for this other person. Queen Ida. Queen Ida was born one weekend in Kerhonkson, New York, at a friend's farm where I got looped on home-made moonshine that my friend's brother, a self-made red-neck bluegrass music producer had whipped up while basting the pig he was cooking in a hole in the ground. Before we left New York for the weekend I had taken off my big toenail, ripped it clear off my foot, while getting out of the shower at our apartment. The pain was the worst I had ever known. My toe was a red, throbbing nerve member that could only throb and be elevated. I could not wear a shoe, and to put pressure on it, as in walk, was excruciating. So we drove up to this pig roast and I hit the moonshine. And then I decided to jump in the lake in the dark, whereupon Jed yelled at me and pulled me out. "You drunken maniac!" I limped around, gathering up my clothes, and put a towel around my head and went to find the family graveyard I had heard wasn't far away. Later that night the host, Brooke, gave me a cane of her grandfather's, and a persona was born: Queen Ida. The cane, the limp, the Hollywood head wrap, the drunken belligerence. The nickname grew faster than the toenail. We talked about her in the third person.

"Queen Ida was out last night," he'd say at breakfast.

"Oh yeah?" I'd say, not looking up from my cereal.

"Yeah. She was a total pain in the ass. She was drooling and eating a chicken wing in bed. And then she thought she was gonna barf. I had to run and get a bucket."

"I'm sure she just didn't eat enough, that's why she got so drunk."

My friends and I took to calling Jed "Grandpa." On a trip to San Francisco we bought him a key chain that said "Grandpa" on it. One weekend we went to California for a wedding and he forbade me to drink the whole weekend. It was honestly the worst weekend of my life.

IT WAS GETTING TOUGH to fit writing into my schedule. Between the drinking and the hangovers, there was just barely enough time to squeeze in sex with my ex-boyfriend and then running around trying to find the perfect turtleneck to wear in April without Jed suspecting I had a hickey underneath. I hated myself. I hated that I lied to someone I really loved. I hated that I wanted better sex than we were capable of having together. I thought if I was a better person I would be okay with mediocre sex. I thought only selfish people insist on fantastic sex all the time. I also thought that creative people must have mind-blowing sex. This was just what they did. Constantly. Sex and art are made from the same source material—insanity. They need hot, hot sex constantly or they become normal, noncreative people. Mostly, though, I couldn't get the writer ex-boyfriend out of my mind. Okay, he was a fitness writer, but he'd gone to Columbia's MFA writing program, briefly, and he was published. And I now lived two blocks from him. And he dedicated his book to me. A book about how to achieve great abs, but it was a bestseller. He was a gay icon, a straight icon, every guy wanted to be Alex. Or at least they wanted to be his stomach. The cover was a giant close-up shot of his sweaty six-pack abs. The dedication read "To Jeanne Darst, for almost killing me but in the end making me stronger." Okay, it wasn't the Great American Novel dedicated to me, but it was the bible of the midsection. How was I to know the second-printing inscription would read "To Natalie Mayer, for almost killing me but in the end making me stronger." I should have known. It's a terrible sign, Nietzsche-paraphrasing, a woman should never ignore this.

Back when we were dating he told me his father was a confidence man and that he worked for his dad selling fake concert tickets over the phone out of hotel rooms in Arizona during summers off from college. Alex was so broke it was ridiculous. For my birthday he gave me a package that consisted of: three library books (was I supposed to return these, or would he?), some hangers, an orange, and a shirt I had left at his house. You better believe the sex was incredible.

I thought, I'm just a terrible person. I have this terrific, kind guy who can give me everything in life and all I want is to screw the abs guy? I was supposed to want marriage and financial stability and a good guy and kids. Other people seemed to be desperate for these things. But I wanted hot sex and the chance to be a writer. And I didn't want to have to lie to get these things.

I told Jed I needed to live on my own, and while we didn't break up, I did move to a dinky place with one window and a sloped floor in the East Village. I did it with money he lent me. In other words I said, "I'm moving out" and "Can you pay for it," in the same breath. No wonder I hated myself.

AT MY NEW PLACE there was a particular album that was making me insane. My neighbor always blared it around four p.m., which is how I deduced he was a bartender. Restaurant and bar shifts start at four-thirty or five p.m. And if they're getting home at six a.m. like he did, they're bartenders, not waitstaff. People who work in restaurants and bars often crank some music as they're getting dressed for work to get them "up" for the long shift. He chose Donna Summer's "Someone Left the Cake Out in the Rain." Real name: "MacArthur Park," one of the all-time worst—terrible lyrics, terrible melody—and he played it every day around four p.m., a time I liked to nap. He wasn't the only noise problem in my building on East Fifth Street in the Village—I wore earplugs to sleep every night—but he was the most dependable. I could hear him on the telephone, could hear him quite loudly if I put a glass against the uneven tenement wall. I never caught actual words, just blathery blather. No one ever came over to his house. Who was this guy?

I was partying a lot with a Scottish woman with whom I worked at Le Gamin. Her daughter lived with the grandmother somewhere upstate because she was unable to care for her. When we were working together we did loads of coke and drank rum during shifts; she was friends with all kinds of models and rockers and actors, maybe she was their dealer, she definitely had a lot of secrets, and she'd get drunk and blather on about her daughter and how much she missed her and then she'd snort up a bag of coke and suggest, "Let's go for a dance at that place on Ludlow Street." It was weird partying with a mother who was unable to take care of her young daughter. I was now the age my mother was when she'd had me, and I felt I was in some kind of cycle that I didn't understand but knew was not good.

I blacked out all the time. I streaked through Tribeca. I thought if I married someone with the kind of money where no one has to work, I might become my mom. This would start with having babies when I barely knew how to take care of myself, and it would go on with drinking with a bunch of babies, and it would continue with not writing, which would make me feel like I hadn't done what I wanted to do. The worst feeling I had as a kid was the feeling that my mother was willing to miss my life for a drink, that she wouldn't stop for me, no matter how much it hurt me, no matter how much I talked to her and worried about her. And I never wanted to make anyone feel like that.

My sober boyfriend was beginning to resemble a giant mirror reflecting back to me my drinking problem. This mirror talked, too.

"I don't know whether you're an alcoholic but you definitely have a drinking problem," he said, in the elevator after the streaking.

"Okay, baby," I said. Anything to end the conversation.

Later at the bar I'd tell my friends about my troubles with Grandpa.

"His sobriety is getting so bad, you guys."

"You don't have to put up with that shit, Jeanne," they'd say.

"I know," I'd say. "I know."

WHEN I QUIT MY JOB at Le Gamin, I lived off of the change that Grandpa threw in this enormous jar in his bedroom. I'd go over when he wasn't home and hit up the jar. I'd wake up and think, What do I need to eat today? Okay, back up, back up: a pack of cigarettes first and foremost, then a coffee, a bagel, maybe a few bucks for a burrito later. The idea of shopping for food for tomorrow was insane to me. Tomorrow? Who knows what's going to happen tomorrow.

One afternoon I had been trying to nap to the tune of "... and I'll never find that recipe again! Oh no!" when I decided I was going to break into the bartender's apartment. I didn't test-market the idea. I just ran with it. The windows in my apartment were odd—sometimes they seemed locked but they weren't. I figured my neighbor's windows might have the same quirk. I got out on my balcony, facing the tenement buildings of East Fourth Street and smoked a cigarette, surveying the scene. Would there be any witnesses? I saw no one on any balconies or in any windows and decided to go for it. I threw my cigarette to the ground and scooted over to his window. I sat for a moment to establish that this was my window and then I reached back and pulled on the bottom of the window. It indeed had the same quirk of unlockability that mine had. I pulled it up really hard and then fell backward through the window, landing on the floor. I was in.

I got up off the floor and looked around. There was just enough light not to need to turn anything on. The head of his bed was up against the window, whereas mine was against the wall. Interesting. Hadn't thought of that furniture arrangement. There was a long table coming out of the wall at the kitchen with a miniature Christmas tree on it. No ornaments but the lights were on. The place was fairly unremarkable. An old *Chorus Line* poster that was in keeping with the Donna Summer thing. He was perhaps a theater major. The difference between the idea of breaking into someone's apartment and the feeling of actually being in an apartment you have illegally entered is immediate. I was in the middle of a crime, a fairly big one, and it was intense but not enjoyable. I wanted to get my business done and get out. What was my business? I saw his wallet on his nightstand. Interesting that he went to work without his wallet. I had lost so many purses, replaced so many driver's licenses and identification after drinking that I now left all ID at home when I went out, too. He had about fifty bucks in his wallet, which I left undisturbed even though I could have used it. I wasn't here to steal anything. I pulled out the driver's license. He was an okay-looking guy, very average, dark blond hair, dark brown eyes, twenty-eight. Footsteps in the outside hallway made me shove the license back in the wallet. I dropped it on the nightstand and ran into the bathroom and got in the shower. The person passed the apartment. It wasn't him. Jesus Christ, I thought. I really need to find a hobby.

The reason I had quit my waitressing job at Le Gamin was that I was starting to lose my mind on people, get in terrible fights with customers, and I thought if I don't get out of this work, "the life" as my father called waitressing, I'll be doing it forever. I had been waitressing for so long it was the only way I knew how to pay my bills. Acting work was not happening. Who knew if I'd ever write anything decent once I actually acknowledged that writing was an act wherein a physical product was produced and not an art of discourse in the vein of the ancient Greeks. From watching my dad I knew how easy it would be for me to become someone who wasn't actually finishing anything. I knew I could either get out (stay out, I should say) or go further in.

Jed was all second-act stuff. He'd kicked heroin, he had money, what was there to figure out? He would have liked to work in film, get bigger theater roles, but these didn't seem to happen for him. He was a wonderful actor, a natural, and this may have been the only pebble in his otherwise clear path of life. It seemed like fighting for something, getting in there and competing, was something he would never even think of doing. Not that it was beneath him, just that it felt disingenuous, given his circumstances. I was terrified of going into this kind of state—a state where to actually want anything seemed insincere, a state of wealth where you needed to always appear grateful, helpful, never desirous. I didn't want to be someone's grateful wife. I didn't want to be a baguette in some asshole's downtown, Ph.D.-fueled, jack-off nonprofit extravaganza. I was probably going to leave the best friend I had ever had.

I got out of the shower and went back into the main room. I didn't take the album. I didn't even think of finding the Donna Summer album and removing it so that he could no longer play it. I just wanted to do one small thing that let him know he was not alone, that there were other people around him. I walked over to the Christmas tree and slid it from the wall to the very end of the table. That should do it. That should let him know he might be drinking too much, he needs to get out more, he should lock his window, he should be more considerate with the '70s disco, he might be losing it. I opened the front door and quickly jumped out, shut his door, opened my own, and went inside to take a nice, peaceful nap.

A ROOM WITH A POO

WHEN JED AND I broke up after five years, I needed to find somewhere affordable to live, so I opted for my sister Katharine and her new husband Henry's couch. I fancy myself a darned good houseguest but after a season or two they got that pained look on their faces. Then they busted me having phone sex on said couch with an actor in Chicago I had done a play with and they asked me to leave. I said farewell to the newlyweds and headed off on my own. I needed to get writing and I couldn't do it with all these leaseholders and apartment owners crowding me. I found something on their street two blocks down. It wasn't exactly an apartment, but then, what was the strict definition of apartment anyway? Some people might insist on amenities like a bathroom, but isn't the expression "Location, location, location"? I've never once heard "bathroom, bathroom, bathroom" when the cognoscenti discuss New York real estate.

Mike and Nicola, the owners, were theater people. I had met them in Austin, Texas, at RAT (Regional Alternative Theater, or Raggedy-Ass Theater) Fest, where theater-makers from

all over the country convened to share info on hijacking bill-
boards, how to sharpen stage pencils at your temp job, this
kind of thing. When I talked to them about moving into two
rooms on the third floor of their brownstone, they informed
me that there was a Puerto Rican family who lived on the second floor and part of the third. The two sisters had lived there
for forty years and as the new owners Mike and Nicola had
no interest in displacing the elderly. As far as Mike and Nicola
were concerned, the two sisters were more than welcome to
die in their building. These two women shared their place with
a fiftyish son and a stoner nineteen-year-old grandson (who,
shortly after I moved out, accidentally shot himself in the face
in his room, approximately ten feet from where I'd been living). Mike and Nicola were far too Brechtian to clear out the
top floors of their home and make more than the two hundred
bucks a month they were likely charging the two sisters.

I learned that before buying the brownstone they had spent
their time in a tepee in a shantytown at the foot of the Manhattan Bridge. The tepee was made of United States government
mailbags sewed together by Nicola. They built a spit outside
where they would roast lambs and things. They siphoned
electricity off a lamppost on the bridge and refused to talk
to journalists who came by, as that would put them back
where they started, on the plane of franchised, connected art-
makers. After about two years, Mike and Nicola felt close,
very fucking close, to closing the gap between them and us,
you and me, him and her, but then in 1993 the city put an end
to the shantytown, razing all of the structures on "the hill."

It was an exciting time for me. I was twenty-eight, and after a rigorous credit check (Mike: "Can you afford four hundred a month?" Me: "I'm sure going to try, Mike"), I got my first very nearly what you would call an apartment. On my own that is. No cosigners, no boyfriends, no sisters. I had two rooms and a sink in a closet. Virginia Woolf would have creamed in her pants. The main room was about twelve feet by twelve. It had two windows that were pretty well rotted through, and wood plank floors, which, with a single weekend of sandblasting, would have been irresistible. Against one wall there was an ancient white stove that looked like it belonged in some old rapist's house in New Hampshire. And then a fridge next to that. This was the kitchen, just a fridge and a stove plunked into a room. There were no cabinets, no counters. If I had to do any fancy culinary moves like slice a tomato, I would put a plate on the stovetop and do it that way. I put a mirror over the sink in the closet. This is where I brushed my teeth, washed my face and peed in the middle of the night when I didn't feel up to using the bathroom in the hall. This is also where I washed my dishes. Outside my door was a roof ladder on which the two old Puerto Rican sisters liked to dry their wigs on hangers after they washed them. I never knew why they chose this spot, right outside my front door, as the place to hang their drying wigs, but this was it and there was no way I could broach this conversation, *en español* or English. Jimmy's door was about ten feet from mine, directly across from my bedroom door. Ignacio (or Nacho, as he was called) and the old aunts were really nice, but Jimmy

I wasn't so sure about. It wasn't just the fact that he was in one of the most diabolical demographics known to man, the eighteen-to-twenty-four-year-old male, it wasn't just the fact that he was a pothead, one of my least favorite addicts. (Potheads being generally lazier and less quick than other addicts. I preferred alcoholics. Alcoholics were charming, snappy dressers, good conversationalists, witty, cynical and a pretty ambitious crowd. Alcoholics were people . . . like me. Heroin addicts displayed tons of derring-do, venturing into abandoned buildings and finding the vein juste, and speed freaks seemed awfully likable, they liked to dance and stay up all night, they patronized the arts, liked to have tons and tons of sex.) It was that Jimmy seemed slightly untrustworthy, which is not a quality you want when sharing a toilet with someone. He was a little slow, like a pubescent Puerto Rican Stanley Kowalski, particularly the way he ordered women around. He had a habit of opening his door around eleven at night and yelling down the stairs, *"Abuela, chocolatay."* A few minutes later his aged grandmother would make her way up the stairs to his door where she would say his name and he would open the door and take the hot chocolate from her and close the door abruptly, never saying thank you. This really got on my nerves, that a nineteen-year-old couldn't make his own hot chocolate.

In the middle of the main room there was a long, light blue couch I had gotten at the Salvation Army. Alongside it was an old mahogany end table that looked like it might have been stolen off a Coachlight Dinner Theater production of

Arsenic and Old Lace. The couch faced a TV atop a white cube between the two windows.

Next to the couch was my desk, where I sat Stegosaurus, my aged Mac, one of those models that had a huge rear and took up your whole desk.

There was a small bedroom that fit only a bed. It had dark gray office carpeting. There was nothing on the walls in either room, a little decorating trick I had picked up from my father, who, since leaving our house in Bronxville, had never hung a single thing on a wall of his apartment. For my dad, walls were the bulletin boards of his mind, where he would tack up thoughts, story ideas, funny things his daughters had said. It was awful to visit him and see some comment you had made about the meaninglessness of work when you were a mother's helper on Nantucket in 1985 on his wall for all to see.

"Do you remember when you said that, Jeanne? Oh, that's a terrific line."

I leaned closer to the wall outside his bathroom door. "'Work is a wonderful spectator sport.' Yeah, I guess I remember that. Seems kinda dumb."

"No, no, a great line! Particularly as it was uttered by a fifteen-year-old mother's helper in a swanky summer WASP hive."

I decided what might be nice for my bedroom was some shelving for my clothes instead of a bureau. As I was clearly walking a new path of an entirely self-made life, I decided to build the shelves myself. I bought a bunch of plywood and nailed the boards together. This did not make shelves. They were more like plywood sculptures that clothing was placed atop. There was no recognizable shelfness to them. If they were the last surviving example of shelving to bring into the future as a prototype, shelves would be extinct.

ONE MORNING I WOKE UP after another big night of drinking and realized that I needed to take an Academy Award–nominated poop. Immediately. I grabbed some sweatpants off my plywood shelf sculpture and pulled them up super-quick. I also spotted a stinky gray running shirt that Julia had given me that was starting to get all holey and thin and pulled that over my head. I dash-dash-dashed into the living room and slipped on my flip-flops. Fuck-fuck-fuck-fuck-fuck I gotta hur-rrrrrrrry. I opened my door and took a step into the hallway and saw the worst sight I could imagine—a closed door. FUCK. SOMEONE IS IN THERE. Mr. Chocolatay, probably. Jesus, Jesus Christ. What was I going to do? I popped back into my room and paced around nervously, trying to gauge how much time I had. Okay, be at the door, stay by the door so you can get in there right when the person comes out. Fuck! Fuck, I am not going to make it. My time is more limited than I thought. Fuck. After some advanced bum clenching there was officially no more time. An executive decision had to be made. I shut my door and darted over to the kitchen area where I looked for something to poop into. The garbage? Yuck. I'm not putting my butt on that gross container. What else? What else? The salad bowl? I like that salad bowl. I need that salad bowl. That's the only bowl I have, actually. There's gotta be something—what else can I—oh, Jesus—bags! Do it in a bag! I grabbed a plastic shopping bag, then realized I'd better double-bag this one, and so I quickly rustled them together, pulled down my sweatpants, hopped over to the stereo and turned NPR up loud for some white-people white noise, and then squatted with the bags pressed up to my ass and put the previous evening behind me. Pulling the bags away from my butt, I thought that, all things considered, Linda Wertheimer, it worked very well. I didn't want to ever have to do that again but the overall result was pretty successful. I felt almost . . . proud, if one can say that about pooping into plastic bags in your living room. Let's not get carried away, that was ridiculously close. I tied the bags together and then tied them together a second time. I didn't want to put them in my garbage. I felt this incident must be disposed of immediately and properly, so I put the bag on the floor and went to get dressed to go out. It was time for a little coffee anyway and I was out of milk. I was sure I could get this day back on track, damn it. I heard whoever was in the bathroom come out. I took off my sweats and threw them atop the shelf sculpture. I put on some white corduroys and slipped back into my black flip-flops. I walked over to the mirror in the closet to check out my tits in the ratty old running T-shirt. Was it still cute to walk around with no bra? Or was I supposed to have some respect for bra rules by this age. Fuck it. Maybe I still got it. Maybe I don't. Today might not be the best day to judge this.

I headed out my door, past the first old Puerto Rican woman's room, where she seemed to be sitting and staring at her refrigerator, then past the pothead's room where a waft of pot came out his half-open door, seeming automated, like a haunted house exhibit. Always in this house doors are open. It's one of the most bewildering traits of the Hispanic people. They could learn a thing or two from white people about the long-standing tradition of closed doors. Why the resistance to hiding things: drugs, drug problems, feelings, accidents? You don't see me pooping into plastic bags with my door half-open, do you? I kept going down the stairs to the second floor where I passed the room of the son, Nacho, seated on a folding chair, drinking a beer, watching a small television, which was sitting on another folding chair. I tried to scurry by unnoticed.

"Hello, Jeanne."

I never got by Nacho unnoticed.

"Hey, Nacho," I said, and quickly kept going with my bag of poop.

One more doorway to get by, the second old Puerto Rican woman. My head was down, but I couldn't help peeking up at the last second to catch sight of her lying on her big double bed. I ambled by with my poop, down the last set of stairs, past Mike and Nicola's apartment.

Out on Dean Street, it was a sunny morning or afternoon. I looked at my watch. Two twenty-five. I didn't want to leave my poop in my own building's garbage so I made a left and headed up Dean toward Smith Street. I was desperate for a coffee. And water. And an everything bagel with cream cheese.

Turned out there was no garbage at the end of my block, so I kept going, sure there would be one at the next block's end. About midway down the block I saw some vague forms in skirts moving toward me, down Dean.

"Hey, Jeanne!" one of the shapes called out to me. It was a publicist named Vera who sat on the board of a nonprofit I was working for, the New York Women's Film Festival, which helped struggling upper-middle-class white women get their films made. Sometimes I wondered whether we shouldn't be helping other people get their films made, like middle-class white women or something.

"Hey, Vera, how are you?"

"I'm well, thank you. Jeanne, this is Martha. Martha is showing me some houses. I'm looking at brownstones in the neighborhood. Do you live here?" she asked.

"Yeah, the middle of the next block down," I answered.

"Really? What number?" Vera asked.

I imagined Vera knocking on my door with a bottle of Merlot, surveying the wet wigs on the hangers outside my door.

"Two-thirty."

"That's so funny! We're looking at two-twenty-nine. That must be directly across the street!"

I became acutely aware that my peers were buying brownstones while I was standing on the street hungover holding a bag of my own feces.

"Wow. I hope it works out. I gotta run, though, I'm late for something." If there was one person I didn't want my shitbag breaking in front of, it was a publicist.

"I'll see you at the board meeting next Monday night. We still don't have mentors for three upper-middle-class filmmakers from Tribeca. I don't know what we're going to do!" She chuckled.

"We'll figure something out at the meeting. See you then." I walked away from them, turning down Hoyt, wondering if my bag had smelled while I was standing there talking. No garbage at the corner of Pacific and Hoyt. Geez. I didn't want to throw it in someone's private garbage because I have had people yell at me for doing this and I was also afraid of someone connecting me with the poop. Finally there was a garbage at the corner of Smith Street and Pacific. I dropped the bag in.

A FEW WEEKENDS EARLIER I had spent the night up at Eleanor's house in Connecticut, and I had to have had about four scotches after dinner, which everyone thought was extremely odd. Apparently I had toddled upstairs and woken up Will, Eleanor's five-year-old, and said good night to him drunkenly. I had recently gotten this very short, very blond haircut which I thought said Jean Seberg or Mia Farrow in *Rosemary's Baby*. The next day Julia said to me, "You better watch out with that new haircut of yours. You're kind of reminding me of someone." She didn't have to say Mom because I had caught it already when I saw myself in the mirror, bombed out of my mind.

What was wrong with me? I put my brain on the problem

every day. I was convinced I had some terrible, terrible disease. Multiple sclerosis, brain tumor, throat cancer. Katharine and Henry had a book at their apartment called *Symptoms*, by Dr. Isadore Rosenfeld, that could take you from chapped elbows to cancer of the spleen in thirty seconds. I would spend hours at their house poring over every possibility of what could be wrong with me. I'm the kind of self-pamperer who will worry I'm going into anabolic shock if I haven't eaten in an hour and a half. I seemed to have a physical imbalance that felt as though it originated in the brain, so brain tumor was a front-runner with tinnitus a close second. The symptoms: hopelessness, unbelievable morning thirst, shame, massive headaches on waking, nausea, profound feelings of regret about things I wasn't sure had actually happened, inability to pay my rent, self-pity, resentment toward the seemingly happy folks of the world, gastrointestinal tropical storms, and self-hatred. One morning I woke up and discovered bruises up and down my right arm. Big bruises. Like someone had punched me. And I remembered I had in fact been punched, repeatedly. By a musician. I thought it would be fun the night before to have a punching contest with this fairly diminutive local Brooklyn drummer. So we traded punches in the arm until I couldn't take anymore. Ha ha. That must have seemed hilarious to us both. The bruises and the swollen arm (which I hid for the week or so it took for them to go away) was a nice mural of what my life had become: a drinker's joke, risky, painful stunts meant to entertain those around me but which felt sad and pointless in the morning. This is why I left Jed? In a weird way I knew that, yes, this was why I had left Jed. For some awkward truth. When you leave a guy as great as Jed you'd better have something magnificent to take its place. I didn't have anything better than Jed and I knew my friends, my family, people I worked with were watching me thinking, This is what you left that nice guy, that nice life for? I left because I was hoping to find some truth about me. But was this it? The truth should feel better, should it not? It should float down from the sky and fit neatly in your little puzzle, you should hear a soft snap when it's in place. Or maybe not.

I spent a great deal of time trying to figure out what disease in particular had a hold on me. Considering how much I smoked, I thought cancer was a tad obvious but a decent bet. Every time I lit a cigarette I imagined throat cancer and voice boxes and I couldn't enjoy smoking anymore. As soon as I put a cigarette out I'd grab a hand mirror and try to see the back of my throat. Red? Lumpy? White spots?

That Monday at the festival office I opened up the *New York Times* and saw that my cousin Thomas French had won a Pulitzer for feature writing in journalism. It was for a series he had written for the *St. Petersburg Times* called "Angels and Demons," about the unsolved murder of three tourists, a mother and her two daughters, in Florida. Brownstones and Pulitzers.

WHEN MY SEASONAL JOB at the film festival ended, I began working for Donato Brunelli, this Hollywood film director who had just moved to New York. Every single photograph in his apartment, where I worked, was of himself with celebrities. Didn't he know anyone—was he not in regular contact with one single person—who wasn't famous? Where were pictures of his parents? Sisters? Brothers?

I was working hard to get to Paris to study with this director named Jacques Lassalle, who had been head of the Comédie-Française, a venerable theater that had been home to Molière. The French embassy had a program where they paid for one or two Americans a year to smoke with theater people in France. I spent months translating my passport and college records, faking my way through interviews in French with various people at the embassy, faxing letters to this very busy director. Often I was so hungover at Donato's that when I would answer the phone and hear the woman at the French embassy who was in charge of my grant, Beatrice Ellis, launching into rapid-fire French I'd have to hang up. She believed I was fluent. I had managed to convince her of this in order to get the grant, but I'm fluent only if I'm the only one talking. The minute someone answers me I'm lost. Perhaps this is how I function in English as well. I was eating all Donato's food and having guys sleep over and showing people his gun and his dildo, which I had found one day. The only highlight of working for Donato was getting to call my childhood hero Evel Knievel once, when Donato was away with various women whose last names he didn't know, to wish Evel a happy birthday. This was the kind of shit Donato thought was normal, having his assistant call to wish you a happy birthday. How thoughtful. Evel didn't seem to notice. Donato asked me to sell his Francis Bacon and I didn't know which painting that was, so I sent the wrong painting to Sotheby's Fall Sale. He'd bark things at me while putting on his jacket to head out the door to the airport like, "Get my L.A. house painted and see if anyone wants to buy it." Slam. Oh. Okay. Any particular color? Oh, and sorry to bother you, but don't you have two houses in L.A.? Because I will sell the wrong house. Office hours were spent at Chinatown pharmacies getting him Valium. And then when he'd go to Los Angeles to shoot a commercial I'd take most of that Valium myself and eat all his fancy-boy food and pass out on his couch.

Finally the embassy accepted me. All I had to do was pay for my flight over there. My happiness was interrupted by Donato, who called me over Labor Day weekend and fired me. It was a classy move, firing me on Labor Day. I didn't have any money to get on a plane. I had no credit cards or extra cash. I was tempted to charge what he owed me, $1,400 for two weeks' work, to his American Express card in dildos and have them delivered to his house.

The next day I got a call to audition for a new Arthur Miller play at the Public Theatre. My life was a mess and nothing ever worked out, but damn if it didn't have some movement.

Apparently this well-known theater director had seen me in a totally wacky play in a barn in Vermont, and he called me in to audition for the American debut of *The Ride Down Mt. Morgan*, a play I knew and liked a lot, about a man who has two wives, two families, who argues that his crime has only resulted in not one happy woman but two. The wives agree with him while hating his guts. It's not Miller's strongest, but it's still good. Patrick Stewart and Blythe Danner were playing the parents of my character. After the initial round of auditions I was brought in to audition for all the people from the Public Theatre and Arthur Miller. This was a really big deal for me. He was going to see what all the bonehead casting directors couldn't and after the show on opening night, when Patrick and Blythe and I were all relaxing with some mai tais at Joe's Pub next door to the theater, Arthur Miller was going to get rather quiet and serious and tell me how to write a decent play. He was tall, probably eighty at the time. I shook his hand and auditioned well. I always regretted not mentioning that as a kid I lived on Stony Hill Farm, where he and Marilyn honeymooned. As I waited to hear from the Public after that audition—it was between me and one other girl—I felt perhaps this was the thing that was going to set me on some ground that was real, not fantasy.

I didn't get the part, who knows why, they never tell you why, and for the next year I drank like a maniac. I couldn't properly support myself, a writer friend died from a heroin and vodka overdose, I endangered a pregnant friend with my Jackie Chan routine on Atlantic Avenue. It was decidedly un-PC, this series of karate kicks and air-chopping with much Asian-accented screaming. I busted it out on some guys on Atlantic Avenue, accidentally almost kicking them in the face and they did not think it was funny and semi-restrained me. The next day I realized my pregnant friend Sara was on the street with us and could have been hurt. I drank alone, I drank after parties, I started going to bars by myself when no one else wanted to drink with me, I got kicked out of bars for drunkenness (this never made sense to me, if you can't be drunk in a bar where can you be drunk? It's like a hospital kicking you out for being too sick). I couldn't control how much I drank or what I said, a lifelong problem that was only heightened when drunk. I frequently hit on the wrong people. I knew women who had sex with oodles of men when drunk, but my dirty secret was that I hit on people not to get laid but to lure them back to my apartment (or usually theirs, as the no-bathroom thing was a hassle to explain), where I would drunkenly spoon them. I was cruising for cuddles. Here's a big moment of clarity as a lady alkie: When guys stop wanting to bang you when you've been drinking, it's a pretty good sign that you have a drinking problem. One night I was house-sitting at a friend's loft on Crosby Street (I did a lot of house-sitting) and this guy I was taking home didn't get out of the cab with me. I was dumbfounded. Look at me. I look so pathetic and dependent I'm almost a tax write-off. And you don't want it?

I knew I wasn't going to beat this thing. I saw that my mother couldn't beat it. I also knew that I would be my own kind of alcoholic. I didn't have any money so I wouldn't be drunkenly ordering from Balducci's and watching *Oprah* while slumped on a divan surrounded by silver riding trophies, brown from neglect, and ashtrays piled high with cigarette butts and peach pits. I'd be that aged temp, that volatile teacher, that "quirky" salesperson at Williams-Sonoma, waiting for five o'clock to get blotto. I was now talking on barstools about all the things I was going to do. And I knew, when the talking starts, things are not good. I was beginning to be able to see myself from the outside. I was trying to be the person talking the shit but I was also the person watching the shit-talker. It was like being out on a date with yourself and knowing you're never going to call yourself after tonight. I was hoping in fact never to run into myself ever again. Katharine says that at the end when I drank I shouted nearly everything. That's what happens after the talking (about all the things I'm going to do) starts, the volume issue. Can everyone hear what an AMAZING person I am? NO? Well, let me try it A LITTLE LOUDER, THEN. I remember being at a party at my friends Brooke and Edgar's house in Park Slope and we were all sitting around their kitchen table, getting drunk as we did, and Edgar was at the fridge asking if anyone needed a beer. I had a cigarette in one hand, half a beer in the other, a glass of whiskey in front of me, a joint was being passed to me and I was waving yes, I need another beer, to Edgar at the fridge. I felt like an alcoholic octopus. If I could have held my glass of Maker's Mark between my toes I would have been swilling that simultaneously. I remember thinking, I can't stop once I start. I can't even slow down once I start. Other people thought I was fun, nutty, entertaining, but I felt defeated and that this feeling would just go on and on. I'd be eking by on seasonal work and peanut butter sandwiches for dinner forever. I saw that no casting director was going to give me a break, that I wasn't capable of being in a relationship, that I was a cheater, that I couldn't support myself. I was going to be left with being a drunk. And that would mean living through the same ordeal twice: first as the daughter of an alcoholic and then as the alcoholic. I couldn't go through those feelings again. For a long time I was worried about becoming my father. Then I was worried about becoming my mother. Now I was worried about becoming myself.

I was thirty years old. I saw the genome on the wall. It read: Beware ye who cross that line into a life of lies and self-deception. You may not make it back. Who would visit this apartment and think I was in good shape? Even my father, king of the depressing domiciles, a man who scribbled the letters of the Greek alphabet on pieces of paper and taped them to his walls so he could engage his brain while using his rowing machine, had a bathroom. I had one fork and one spoon and two knives. I had a couple plates and three mugs. I had one blanket and a purple sleeping bag Jed had bought me for a camping trip. It was super-warm and nice, but every time I stuffed my feet into that little pocket at the bottom I thought, I need a decent comforter. This is pretty depressing.

I was trying to get help. I was seeing a shrink in therapyville, the highly concentrated area of downtown therapist offices between Fourteenth Street and Eighth Street from University Place to Fifth Avenue. Hildey was great. Very motherly, and I needed that at first. She was about fifty and very gentle. She was cheap and when I couldn't afford cheap she let me run a tab with her. We talked a lot about my mother and how difficult it was to watch her give up on herself, how she was seemingly rehab-proof, how she was a total shut-in now, having all her booze delivered, how she looked, how she smelled, how awful it was to mourn someone while they are still alive. Hildey was a great listener and remembered things I said long past the point when I thought it was charming to be quoted directly by your therapist. But she just kept pushing a regular job on me, kept trying to get me to see how being a writer was this terrible, terrible thing. I think that as a regular person she just couldn't understand all the dumb shit I did and the pathetic ways I got by, scraping by on no money, never going to the doctor or the dentist, calling my painter friend Linda who was equally broke to come with me when I needed to go to the bank to check my balance, for moral support. This was probably an unsettling thing for Hildey to witness. Things weren't going well for me, I wasn't denying that, but I was doing what I wanted to despite the number of times I opened mail and saw the words "overdue," "past due," and "delinquent." She didn't understand I didn't want the stockbroker hubby and the framed photo of Ronald Reagan in his ranch hat over the bed. I had had the opportunity for a regular life, to be a missus, and had decided that that was not going to get my word count up. She didn't understand this was what being an artist looks like, disaster, total personal ruin. God. Get with it, lady.

"Jeanne, I think you're a wonderful person with a family history that can only be described as 'chilling,' and I'm trying to get you to see how you can utilize your talents in a healthy way."

"There's no healthy way to use talent, Hildey."

It seemed she was always trying to get me to give up the only thing I had, the only thing that gave meaning to my life.

Hildey had some issues of her own that were annoying but not deal breakers. Hildey had Lyme disease and had trouble keeping weight on, so she snacked discreetly during our sessions. I saw nothing wrong with this. I did, however, think it was odd that she answered the phone during my sessions, and when I suggested she get an answering machine she balked as if she wasn't one of those techie people. An answering machine in 1999 was hardly cutting-edge. Most New York City chipmunks had them at the time. It had been weeks since I asked her to get one, and she was still picking up the phone when it rang.

"I'm sorry, Jeanne, but I have to be available to patients. What if it's a real emergency? Fifty minutes is too long to wait."

I would grumble and go on.

One day she let me know she was having some Lyme-related procedure at the hospital the following day and she would need to pick up the phone if the hospital called.

I told her that was fine, and on my end I might have some feelings about her picking up the phone and these feelings might lead to some actions. "Just so you know," I told her. She nervously put some leftovers into the microwave that she shared with the other therapists down the hall, and came back in and closed the door.

About twenty minutes into the session her phone rang. She looked at me as if to say, "I have to get this." I gave her my best death stare, really put some effort into this and into maintaining it for the whole phone call, which was three or four minutes. I was doing really well, she looked incredibly scared of me, when a strange small explosion sound in the hall happened, followed by people murmuring, "Looks like chicken vindaloo." "No, more like a regular yellow curry." "Wow. Whose food is that?" "What a mess."

Hildey opened her door to wave at the other therapists and let them know it was her mess, she'd deal with it, and then the person on the phone audibly screamed something. Hildey said, "I have not called you twenty times today, I need to know what time the procedure is tomorrow. I am not bothering you," and she looked at me and just started bawling right there in her little therapist's office. I was totally taken aback. The death stare melted into a shocked zombie.

The other therapists headed off in a clump back to their offices as if they might catch what she had. Hildey ended her phone call and slumped in her chair, weeping. I didn't want to comfort her or even deal with her but I also didn't want to be mean and ignore her, so I got my bag and said, "I guess I'll see you next week, Hildey," and I headed to the elevator.

I walked out onto University Place wondering why all the people who were supposed to be in the stability biz—mothers, fathers, therapists—fell apart on me.

The next week I went back, and Hildey wanted to talk about what had happened like it was some kind of international incident. Each week after that I was meaner and meaner to Hildey. I couldn't help it. She wasn't capable of doing her job. She lost her shit. Maybe she should have taken a day off.

"I think the transference has gone bad, Jeanne. Between therapist and patient," she said to me one day.

"Oh, really? I think I might know when that happened. It might have been the moment you became my mother and I had to comfort you while you cried and charged me and cried and charged me. Bad as things may have been with my mother, she never charged me. Angry? Why, yes, I am, Hildey! Is there a problem with that? Anger is not just important to me. It's essential. I need it. In my relationships with men, my father, my mother and to turn into material, frankly. Why is everybody so down on anger when to me, it's so bloody practical."

I never saw Hildey again, and what eats at me is I probably owe her some money. But then I think, Okay, I owe her for three sessions, but she cried at one and the other two we talked about how I felt about her crying on me, so do I actually owe her anything?

I tried talking to Julia about how I felt like blowing my head off. We had dinner, and when I said as much she threw her glove at me, hitting me in the face. I'm not entirely sure why she did this. I then threw my glove at her, and then the miso soup arrived.

One night I listened to Nina Simone and drank grappa I had stolen from my father. I called my friend Cassie from college who lived in Aspen and was an acupuncturist. Her life had seemed to just get better and better in the last few years, at the exact rate that mine was getting worse and worse. She was doing what she wanted to do, she kept making more and more money, she was making $90,000 a year, while I was buying loaves of bread and jars of peanut butter as the cheapest way to make it through a week. I would babysit my niece and bring my laundry over, use my sister's detergent, and take things to eat later that I knew they probably wouldn't miss: one PowerBar, three bags of mint tea, some small boxes of kid-sized raisins, an apple, a hunk of cheddar. I always wanted to take coffee but it would smell too much, wafting out of my backpack. I classified this behavior as advanced mooching, something I was doing because I didn't have time to go to the grocery store—that was what boring, married people with kids did. I was too edgy for the grocery store. Please.

Cassie was cheery and hopeful and she looked a hundred times better than me, she was traveling through Asia in the off-season and just loving everything all the time. I had no idea that she was sober, I just knew that she was a big pain in the ass whenever she came to New York.

"Can I bring anything to the party?" she'd ask.

"Beer."

"What about something else?"

"Nope, just beer."

She'd show up with flowers after this exchange, and I assumed she was just too lazy to carry a few six packs from the deli. Or I figured she was doing some kind of cleanse.

I was also pretty sick of her wanting to go to dinner all the time when she visited. Who had money for dinner? Insanity.

I normally didn't talk to Cassie about my problems, because her shelves were nothing but self-help books, full of slogans like "Love yourself through disappointment" and "Feel your feelings!" Over the course of our friendship I had never contracted a slogan or an issue or a boundary or any sense of hope or cheerfulness, so I figured out it was safe to hang around these kinds of people. On the phone I went through the litany of things that were making me feel like killing myself and then, out of nowhere, I said, "And I'm working on a little drinking problem here." She told me she had been sober for three years (that's what that was?) and maybe I needed to get sober. Well, sure, maybe I needed to do a lot of things: quit smoking, do some actual writing, get a bathroom, get a job. Doesn't mean I'm going to do any of them.

"Why don't you try and not drink tomorrow?" she suggested.

I couldn't believe my life had dried up to the point of taking advice from a woman who once scribbled and left a note on a sleeping homeless man on the F train that read "You matter." A woman who had only a few years before invited me to her graduation from a self-help program called LifeYes!, where we met all the graduates in a hotel ballroom in midtown and they all had their eyes shut as "Greatest Love of All" played. When Whitney shut up, they opened their eyes, and you, their friend, stood in front of them as they all sobbed uncontrollably about you weren't sure what. Self-help was a bad, bad place as far as I was concerned. The term itself was bad. It wasn't helping yourself, it was just the opposite. If you could help yourself you wouldn't be in a ballroom with all these other losers, you'd be home, solving your problems. Why didn't they call it "can't help self" or just "fucking help me"?

I also disliked the word "recovery," despised the "language

of the heart," and recovery slogans. It all reminded me of those posters in the high school guidance counselor's office: a picture of a kitten on the end of a rope with "Hang in There!" underneath. It reminded me of secretaries with little notes posted around their desks to get them through the weeklong fake laugh of office life. People who needed little pictures of monkeys skateboarding and toddlers walking down a hall in high-heeled shoes were probably the same people who went to church and went on "journeys" all the time. The same people who thought everything happens for a reason. Dumb people. The only self-help book I saw in our house was *I'm OK, You're OK*, which lived in a drawer of Mom's night table, like a hotel Bible, untouched. That and *The Inner Game of Tennis* were about as deep into self-help reading as my parents went. The aesthetic of sobriety was "god-awful," my mother would have said, no style at all, no "flair." Half their friends had been electroshocked when they couldn't get their shit together. Maybe after going to Catholic schools and then seeing the Democratic vice presidential nominee and family friend Thomas Eagleton and other friends torn to shreds for admitting depression, my parents felt the only thing worse than alcoholism and depression was to get help for them.

The thing is, I had no other options. A few days later I said out loud, "I'm an alcoholic." And I felt like it was the first honest thing I had said in my life. Like the last thing I ever wanted to say. It made me nervous but I knew it was something I had been looking for my whole life. Not sobriety of course, but the truth.

I thought, Well, if I'm considering killing myself here, maybe I'll give this sobriety a chance. I always thought I would drink less, drink better, stop slugging people when I got my shit together. I drank because of my problems and once those went away I wouldn't drink so much. But I agreed to reverse the logical order of things and quit drinking first in order to get a handle on those problems. Not for a lifetime. Just to solve my problems with a clear head, and then I could drink normally again . . . or, you know, for the first time.

I DIDN'T TELL ANYONE I wasn't drinking, because if I couldn't do it, I didn't want anyone to know I had wanted one more thing and couldn't hack it. And if I didn't ultimately want to quit drinking, I wanted to go back to drinking in peace without being teased endlessly about the time I said I was quitting. My whole life had felt like a good story—something in which I participated in order to create something that could be used for conversation later. Was I using what had happened in my life to create art or was I *making* things happen to create art? This got harder to stomach: "Jeanne, tell the story about the boss who tried to kill you with the lead pipe!" Be entertaining. Stories. For the benefit of others. How did people latch on to emotionally healthy people? They seemed elusive, like trying to scale a smooth interior wall of a museum. How would anyone latch on to me? In "The Jelly-Bean," Jim Powell loved Nancy Lamar because she was a disaster, a fun, free-spirited, beautiful disaster. No one loves a sane girl. At least they didn't in my house.

Whether I succeeded or failed at quitting drinking it was going to be my success or my failure.

Things were worse than before I quit drinking. I was now living in a couple rooms with wigs drying on a hanger outside my front door and a restless, unpredictable teenage pothead next door and no bathroom and no money, no job, no ascertainable work skills, all without alcohol. This was much worse. I knew I couldn't be around my friends at first because I knew if they asked, "Darst, what are you drinking?" I would have just burst into tears.

So when Cassie called again and said, "Why don't you come get sober out here in Aspen? You have nothing going on there," I said I'd be out there in two days.

SOBER SCHMOBER

I'M NOT THAT BIG on dreams, telling other people about them, interpreting them, the symbols. Pretty boring stuff. When I hear "I had the weirdest dream last night . . ." I usually give the throat-slash sign to the speaker. I had a recurring dream for about fifteen years that I never told anyone about for the aforementioned reason. It wasn't noteworthy. Until I stopped having it. In the dream I would fall down, often roll down a hill, and come to the bottom, and I couldn't get up. My legs wouldn't work right and I was weak and unable to stand up. And in the dream I desperately wanted to get up but couldn't. I would fall down every time I tried to stand. When I quit drinking I never had the dream again.

In Aspen, I got a job as a driver for a limo company, driving luxury SUVs. I had a black Denali. My first day as I was backing out of the garage I took off the sideview mirror. I thought, I hope they don't give me a lot of shit for this, seeing as I'm the only woman driver here on the force. A second later I heard one of the guys yell to the manager in the office, "Yup, that was the girl!"

A lot of the runs were from the Aspen airport to the St. Regis hotel in town. It was an easy drive; Aspen is not midtown Manhattan. I kept getting reprimanded because I would pull into the semicircle driveway of the St. Regis and my Denali would be a good three feet from the curb. This was apparently the mark of an amateur. A good driver would get the car right up against the curb for his passengers. Maybe now was not the time to tell my employers that I hadn't even taken my own road test, that my sister Julia took it for me. One day my supervisor, Tad, was in a car ahead of me in the St. Regis driveway and he hopped out of his Denali and came over to my vehicle and said, "Hey, Jeanne, when you have a second, like when you're waiting for a client, it's a great time to do a little maintenance on your vehicle. Like, why don't you hop out, grab a rag and wipe down your vehicle?"

"Because someone might see me?"

A few days later I picked up my assignment sheet for the day and saw that one of the runs out of the airport was Deepak Chopra at twelve forty-five. Cassie thought I was the luckiest person alive; she almost wished she were me for half a second. This could be a real turning point for you and listen to what he has to say and ask him what you're supposed to be doing with your life, don't be negative, be present for the experience and all this "Everything happens for a reason" caca. I was more concerned with not winding up in a ravine with the guru than I was with understanding what the reason is why I couldn't drink anymore and now had to drive people to and from airports. Naturally I had no idea what this joker smoker looked like, so I made a little DEEPAK CHOPRA sign and stood at the gate with it. The whole plane had deboarded after about fifteen minutes. There was nowhere else he could be; the airport is teeny. Then four giant black men, New York Giants it turned out, came toward me. I lowered my Deepak sign.

"Are you our ride?" one of them said.

"Yes, yes, right this way," I said, forgetting to ask if I could carry anything for them. I turned back.

"Do you have luggage?" I asked.

"No, missy, it's your lucky day," one of them said. They were laughing at me but I didn't take it personally. They were Giants.

We headed out to the car. I opened the back to put their carry-ons in.

"Let me take those," I said, looking at their big bags.

"Oh, give me a break, girl," and they laughed, hoisting their bags into the back. I was relieved. The drive to the St. Regis was uneventful. I felt fairly competent as we cruised out of the airport; I remembered the speed bump on the way out and slowed accordingly, saving me from having to apologize for bumping their heads. I felt like a good driver. I was certain I was going to nail the curb thing this time, too.

The Giants remarked that the village looked like "fuckin' Hansel and Gretel town," which was true. They wondered how much "cheddar you gotta have to have a house here." They guessed "Will Smith cheddar," and then I got sort of near the curb and dropped them all off. I headed back to the garage. My boss was waiting for me as I pulled in.

"Jeanne, what happened to Deepak Chopra?" Bob asked.

"I don't know."

"Well, I do. There was nobody there to meet him at the airport and after standing around waiting for one of our guys for twenty minutes, he took a cab. A cab. To his hotel."

I thought that didn't seem like the worst thing that could happen to someone. I mean, if anyone should be able to handle this it's Deepak fucking Chopra. But my boss didn't see it that way. I hopped on the thirty-year-old yellow ten-speed that Cassie had coaxed her landlord into letting me use for the summer, and rode to the supermarket for a newspaper. I was going to need another job.

I had had clear skin my whole life, but when I quit drinking I got this weird acne. (Who knew all that beer and Maker's Mark was making my skin look so fabulous?) Despite looking horrible, I managed to find someone to spoon my boils, this former drug addict mechanic in Aspen, Sam. Sam couldn't remember anything. His whole life was a blackout and he was pretty sensitive about it so I tried to keep questions like "Do you like mustard?" to a minimum. Sam looked at me with amazement when he saw me after we'd been apart a day or two, and I was convinced he eyed me with such delight because he'd actually forgotten about me and so it was like meeting me for the first time every time we went out, like every day was a Christopher

Nolan movie for him. "Hey there . . . beautiful." Sam lived at his shop across from the airport. The garage was packed with cars he was working on and outside were a zillion cars waiting to be worked on. He lived above the garage, an area you got to by climbing a ladder. There was a makeshift kitchen he and the other mechanics used with a fridge and a microwave, and Sam would toddle down there at night after we'd fool around and come back up the ladder with a pint of ice cream.

Like Sam, I didn't know how to do anything, and the biggest shock of early sobriety was how uncomfortable I really was, how reliant on alcohol. I hoped my entire being wasn't dependent on alcohol to operate: my sense of humor, my brain, my ability to talk to people and the pleasure I took in meeting new people. I hoped some normal person would emerge out of all this, me, that I was still in there, but there was no way to predict if that was true—if I would become someone different, or just a sober, less violent version of myself. After about four months it was time to answer this question by getting back to my regular life.

When I got back to Brooklyn, the first party I went to sober was at a good friend's house in Park Slope, the place where I had partied and eaten dinner and lunch and hung out endlessly, often sleeping over even though I lived nearby because I couldn't make it home. I was chatting with someone I didn't know, someone who in my former life would have been mere set-dressing, as people were when I drank, and I poured myself a seltzer and sipped and talked uncomfortably. I had the distinct feeling that something was missing from my drink, alcohol obviously, but surely there was something I could put in my seltzer that would jazz it up, so I reached for a banana on the counter, pulled down the peel and sliced a big piece of it on a plastic cutting board and dropped it in my seltzer. The woman I was talking to said, "Did you just put banana in your seltzer?" and I looked down at my drink and defensively shot back, "Yes," as if she were completely unaware of drink trends.

"SO YOU'RE JUST on wine now, is that it? That seems very smart," my father says when I tell him I'm sober.

"No, Dad. No wine, no—"

"I think that's a fine idea. Stick to beer."

"No beer, Dad, nothing—"

"A good beer is just as well. Might even try that myself."

"YOU SEE I LIKE to have one gin and tonic on summer nights," Eleanor confides on a warm summer night sitting on her back lawn in Connecticut when I tell her I'm sober. "That's why I never overdo it. Ever. Because I like to have one drink on summer nights sitting outside."

"That's great. But, I've already overdone it so I can't have anything."

"That's why I never overdid it."

"Well, I did."

"Okay, okay. Do you want a . . . juice box?"

DESPITE WHAT ALL the triumphant recovery movies and books might have you believe, it's possible to get sober and have nobody really give a shit. So our lives have been ravaged by alcoholism for the last twenty years. What is it that you want me to say?

I HAD COFFEE with Julia around this time and I apologized for the way I had treated her when I was drinking. She said, "Big fucking deal, Jeanne. You're a total psycho, drunk or sober."

I NEEDED TO SEE Grandpa (Jed). If we had broken up because I was a lushy mess and he was sober, my mind told me there was now a new equation, math even I could get, a simple fraction: sober/man = sober/woman. I was now, well, pulling my weight in the equation of our love. I went over to his house to announce the good news, the news of my return to him. He made me a peanut butter and jelly sandwich and a coffee and listened.

"This is the best news I've gotten in a long time," he said.

"So, I mean, I thought we could give it another shot—"

"Another what? Another shot? Are you crazy?" He lit a cigarette.

"Now that I'm sober," I reminded him.

"Listen, I want you to have the happiest life you can possibly have. I want you to have everything you ever wanted"—he gestured with his hands—"over there. Like way over there."

"You wanted to get married."

"Yeah, well, that's before we broke up. I had no idea how happy I was going to be without you. Which is why I'm not mad about all the shit you pulled—the roast beef sandwiches you ate drunk out of your mind in our bed, the time you were drunk and tried to stick that long-stemmed rose up my ass, the cheating, none of it. Because you were the one who ended it and for that I will always owe you."

"Look, you don't have to answer now. Maybe you want to take some time to think about what it would be like with me sober now—"

"No. Nope. No way."

I finished my PB and J and we smoked a cig together and I took a look around at the old luxury SoHo loft and left.

MY MOTHER WASN'T IMPRESSED or amazed and she didn't want to know how I'd done it or when or what it was like or was it difficult or how did I feel now. She probably thought I was pretending to be sober to get her sober. I don't know. We didn't talk about it much.

Being sober is the most important thing to me, and yet I really hate people who blab on and on about being sober and how they did it and why they're so much better than people who can't get sober. Alcoholism is horrible and all alcoholics would like to get good and stinky regularly if they could. What people who get sober don't talk about is that sobriety can be monotonous, can feel like your personality is living in a gated community, that sometimes it's hard to access fun and wildness because it might be located in the same region of your brain that says, "Have four hundred beers right now and then show someone your butt!" I don't like feeling so protective of myself. Some sober people do a lot of processing and healing and going on journeys, and that stuff doesn't feel like the most fun, it feels like self-obsession, overthinking life, instead of living. I'm sure that I'm meant to be sober. But that doesn't mean that I always want to be sober.

I never know what to drink. "What'll you have?" is such an absurd question to me now. What'll I have? Well, I can't have anything, if you want to know the truth. Bring me whatever you want. It doesn't matter. I'm sober. None of it's gonna be any fun.

But being sober was this amazing trip into regular life, what normal people do every day—pay their phone bills, get stains out of shirts, poo in toilets—an adventure in normalcy. One morning I woke up and made coffee and realized that I had no milk. I was annoyed that I'd have to go out so early and get milk and just as I was shutting the fridge I saw a brown bag I had gotten the night before. I opened it, amazed, delighted, baffled. Backup milk! I had bought backup milk! I am so fucking sober it's crazy!!! I want major awards for doing stuff normal people do all day long. If I'm at my sister's and I'm helping clean up after dinner I want acknowledgment for not being a fuckface. "Do you SEE ME? Do you SEE me wiping this table? Pretty amazing, right?" I'll knock over a lamp while dusting if I think I'm not being noticed being helpful. I find myself phoning friends if I'm walking to a mailbox to mail some bills.

"Hey, Linda, it's Jeanne. Thought I'd call and say hi. I'm just mailing my Con Ed bill on Court Street. Call me back, I'll tell you all about it."

And as I walked around without a hangover I realized I could do some writing now. I was physically able to do it unlike when I was drinking. Maybe I could manage a few words just on cigarettes. And yes, the Hemingways, the Fitzgeralds, the Faulkners and the Capotes. Drank while writing. Drink next to the typewriter. But the longer I lived in Brooklyn, the more writers I met, and I guess I was just too drunk to put it together before but now I realized about half of them were sober. So you *could* be a writer and be sober. Very interesting.

A SALLY OF THE MIND

I WAS WORKING in a coffee shop in Brooklyn and got a call from a guy who had done the women's film festival website and was now a vice president at Sundance Channel. He liked the writing I did for the festival's website and catalog and offered me my first real job, working for Sundance Channel. I was going to get paid to be a writer. I knew getting paid and being good had nothing to do with each other, but that didn't mean it didn't feel great. It was a full-time job. I had a name-plate on my office door with the word WRITER underneath it.

But my first real job confirmed a hunch I'd had for a while: I don't want a real job. The job was great. It really was. I could go have a cig downstairs, make a phone call without being "on a break." I could take lunch when I felt like it. Adult. Professional. I wrote for the website, interstitial promos, and for two actual film shows. Being a normal person was a lot easier than what I'd been doing for the last decade—but being normal was scary because it seemed like, if I go down this road who knows what will happen to me? It's just not safe for an artist to blend into the working world. I could, well, I could get used to it for one thing. I was starting to buy "work clothes," aching for sweaters that would look right for the Monday staff meeting, so my thrift store old man sweaters wouldn't, you know, draw attention to me.

I was able to move to a studio a few blocks away with a bathroom. Nothing fancy but a regular apartment. I had no credit or credibility so I couldn't rent an apartment on my own. I got it by just moving my stuff in when a friend was moving out. I had a real job and a real apartment. Which let me tell you felt . . . boring.

Some people I knew, dancers, writers, painters, did work like answering phones in day spas or something completely unrelated to their interest or talent, saving their mental energy for their own creative work. I also knew writers who worked in something related, like an ad agency, and then came home and wrote their book at night. These people liked to do something for money that "uses their brain." I fell into the "not using your brain for work" category. When I went to work at a cable TV station I felt like someone who works at a cable TV station, and not like someone who was doing this in order to go home and write.

One day at Sundance, I got a call from Dad, who had moved from the West Village to Brooklyn a few years earlier, just around the corner from me and Katharine and Henry. He had taken over the apartment that Julia was leaving, because it was a lot cheaper than his place on West Fourth Street. He lived there a short while until he decided to move in with my mother again. I don't know how they'd cooked up this idea but they had thought it was a winner: he got to save money and she got an *"au père"* of sorts, a father of her children to take out her garbage and answer the door when the liquor store delivery guy came by. They lasted about six days, until the night Dad went out to get an ink cartridge for his printer and when he came back Mom had bolted the inside lock and wouldn't let him back in, not even to get his things. That's when he called me. He came and slept on the blue couch in my living room and for the next few days we were roomies. While at my house, he asked what I was reading, what I was writing, and I lied about both, pretending to be very diligently "on" a play. He told me what he was reading and lied about what he was writing. We talked about day jobs and money problems and joked that jail would be a wonderful place to get some work done, three meals a day served to you, no preparation time, get a lot of reading done, a little exercise to keep the mind sharp, no rent to worry about, no distractions except the occasional visit from a loved one. Then he went to Katharine and Henry's for a few nights, and then he slept at Eleanor's until he found a new place in Brooklyn.

This could have been the moment when I said, Wow, do I want to be sleeping on some couch of my kid's when I'm sixty-seven? I got it good. I gotta hang on to this job thing or it's back to peeing in sinks for me. But instead, I quit.

I left partly because in a staff meeting one day I couldn't remember what our actual product was. We were talking about the website routing people to the channel, which routed people to our magazine, which directed viewers to the news show we aired about the shows on the channel, and I thought, I can't be the only person in this room who can't keep straight what we sell. When I quit, the reactions from people who'd watched me be broke all my life were quite dramatic. I suppose just because you quit drinking doesn't mean you know how to do stuff—keep a good job, or do things that make sense. But the way I saw it, I needed to get back to crummy jobs, only this time I would write while working these crummy jobs.

I got a job working at a friend's high-end modern furniture store and art gallery. I wrote humor pieces and a profile of a former WPA sculptor who hung around the store. I wrote a lot of my own stuff. Then my friend got a permanent employee so I had to find another job. That was September 10, 2001. There was now no work available, crummy or not so crummy. Nothing. Over the next seven months I sent out résumés for hundreds of jobs—receptionist at an animal clinic, where I would have to wear colorful scrubs with kittens on them; a job signing people up for long-distance phone plans at college campuses; part-time nanny; assembler of boxes for shipping art; ESL teacher at a women's center—knowing I would never get those jobs. There were no jobs for anyone in New York. I was about to get evicted but I was halfway through writing a play. Maybe I did need poverty and instability to write.

It didn't seem to be a successful recipe for Dad, though. I was watching him make do with less and less, and I didn't know whom to worry about. My dad, my mom, myself. My dad was offered a full-time permanent job by a law firm as a kind of impeccable in-house grammarian. He must have been sixty-eight when he was offered this job, but he turned it down because he was getting "very close" with the Fitzgerald book. The whole family was astounded that this book project was still going strong. It was stronger than his desire for a regular paycheck, which would mean it was stronger than his need to know his rent would be paid, stronger than food, a movie here and there, dinner out with his daughters and grandkids, a cab in the rain. It seemed there was nothing more important than "the project." And it was always almost there. It was more than a decade at least at this point. "A few months at the outside and it's ready." I knew what he was doing looked crazy to everyone else and it looked crazy to me, too. But I had just done the very same thing. Left a really good job. My mind could say, "That is crazy behavior. Fantasy. Delusion." My soul, however, said, "That's what we do. That is just what we do."

I HAD NO IDEA how to help him. He was in total denial that he even needed help, but he ate almost everything off our plates at restaurants. For our birthdays we always got a check from him that he'd tell us to "wait a couple days on that one, would you?" And the birthday girl would wait and ask a few days later if it could be deposited. "Better hold off a day or two just to be sure," until eventually it became like an acting exercise, pretending the check was something other than a piece of paper. Sometimes I would see my father a couple blocks down Court Street, coming out of a bakery with a loaf of bread under his arm, and I would turn the corner. It was too painful sometimes to talk to him, he seemed like a real-life Court Street tragic hero/figure. Like running into King Lear outside his Clinton Street walk-up. He may not have enough work, enough, God forbid, to eat, and my life was no different.

I WAS NOW THREE MONTHS behind on rent. Was this a good time to write a play or a bad time to write a play? My friend in Vermont who runs a theater company in an old barn offered me an August spot to do a show. I took it. It wasn't the first time I had accepted an offer to perform a play that had yet to be written. I sublet my place and headed to Warren, Vermont, to live in a trailer in the woods and finish this play.

I stayed in a 1954 Prairie Schooner trailer that the owner, an architect at a university in Seattle, had made into a crazy compound with an Airstream down the hill and a wood deck and French windows. A stonemason had built a beautiful stone wall around the trailer. There was an outdoor shower off the back of the trailer. The main attraction, though, was the glass outhouse in the woods. It was a compost toilet and his girlfriend, a Seattle artist, had put broken plates all over the front of it. It had amazing views of the mountains. I called it the Julian Schnabel outhouse. People were always coming by from local colleges and environmental building classes to check out the famous glass compost outhouse. And they never called first, so I'd be out there using it and crowds of design/build geeks would come over the hill and find me there in my bathroom.

In the trailer in Vermont, I managed to finish the play about a prostitute named Sally who was raised on a commune in Northern California, started by her father, where they grow endive and wear old fencing clothes discarded from the California College of Arts and Crafts. She moves to New York City as a teenager after all the kids are kicked off the commune by the father. She becomes a sex worker in the meatpacking district but decides, amid all the art world craziness of the '80s in New York, that what she does is actually art, that her fucking is so rich, so expressive, that she's a "fucking artist." She adapts Orwell's *Animal Farm* into a blow job and collaborates with a man who calls himself Ken Burn on a seventeen-part PBS series called *The American Anus*. She stops charging people and becomes a full-time fucking artist and sets up a nonprofit. She eventually winds up experiencing a Thoreau-style look back at her life, minus eating woodchucks. She thumbs through the Bible one day, specifically the Sermon on the Mount, which she decides is Jesus' one-man show, and she thinks, Well, if John Leguizamo and Eric Bogosian and now Jesus can do one-person shows, why can't I? So Sally writes her one-woman show and calls it *Sally on the Mount*. I performed it in the barn at the end of the summer. As Sally, I change clothes onstage, climb on pianos in high-heeled hiking boots, sing badly. It's fun.

Sally started as a way to avoid getting evicted from my apartment on Amity Street. But when I got back from Vermont, I still owed rent and was evicted anyway. I had to have two friends come over and pack all my things in the middle of the night and help me get them to my new apartment in Park Slope, before the sheriff arrived in the morning to put a lock on my door.

Shortly after I moved into this new place with a roommate, the economy started to pick up and I got a bunch of little jobs. I freelanced for a branding company: two hundred bucks and a catered breakfast for a three-hour workshop to come up with ideas for new products and snappy language for old products—a great gig. There were not enough workshops to survive on, though, so I also worked at a vintage clothing store in Brooklyn, for nine dollars an hour. I picked up my niece, Louisa, a couple days a week from school and baby-sat at night. I read books and wrote reading guides for HarperCollins. I was always scrambling for more work, always late on rent and often just plain out of money. Once, after concluding a workshop at the branding company, I was too broke to take the subway home and too chicken to jump the turnstile. I was so tired of being the loser, the mooch, always borrowing from my sister Katharine. I could have called and said, "Can you loan me ten bucks," but there is something—I know this from my father's borrowing—something even sadder about borrowing a small amount of money than a large one. Ten bucks is a sad sum. A thousand bucks is understandable somehow. A million bucks is downright dignified. So I walked from Thirtieth and Seventh, just down from Madison Square Garden, to Berkeley Place in Park Slope, about six miles. Most people in New York do this only when radical Islamists fly planes into the World Trade Center. I walked everywhere. I have always liked to walk, but I also *had* to walk everywhere I went. I needed every dollar.

One month when I couldn't pay rent at my new, cheaper Park Slope pad I devised a financial plan of a rent reading. I decided to read *Sally on the Mount*, which had been staged only once at the barn in Vermont, in my apartment living room. Katharine made brownies. We gave away beer and charged people ten bucks. In three nights I made over eight hundred bucks, which was my rent. The reaction to the play was really good, good enough to make me decide the play should be produced. I brought it back to the barn in Vermont that summer as a more finished work. Then it went to the Lower East Side, then Hawaii, then Puerto Rico over Christmas. Never went near a theater. Halfway through the run at Tonic, a jazz place on the Lower East Side, I got a grant for seven thousand bucks. My work for the first time felt real. I was a playwright. It wasn't easy and it wasn't pretty but it wasn't a fantasy, either.

IT TAKES A
WEST VILLAGE

MY MOTHER OFFICIALLY DIED of a stroke. It's difficult to detect when alcoholics are having the small strokes that precede a larger, deadly stroke because often people assume they're just drunk. My father had spoken to her a few times that week and nothing seemed terribly wrong. When he went to her apartment to do the little things he did for her he found her on the floor unconscious. By the time the ambulance got her to St. Vincent's she was in a coma and was almost immediately pronounced brain dead. I had called her a few days earlier, on Valentine's Day, but got a busy signal. For some reason that was our day. On Valentine's Day she felt like my mom, which was not always the case with my birthday or Christmas. On Valentine's Day she felt like the woman who cried with me watching *Little House on the Prairie* after school ("God damn that Half Pint!" she'd say, reaching for a cigarette), the woman who'd pretended to tie me up to the radiator after we watched *Sybil* together one Sunday afternoon, the woman who loved to smoke and watch the US Open and ogle Vitas Gerulaitis.

I was in Los Angeles doing my play when I got the same phone call I had been getting for about seventeen years: "Your mother is about to die." But she never did. But this time she did.

Katharine and Julia and I were here to deal with all of it, to throw it out, give to Goodwill, leave for the super, divide among ourselves, and with the things no one wanted to keep, sell, or leave, bring to my dad's. Eleanor would come with Jim the following day to clean the place up the best they could.

There were mouse droppings in corners and on tables and worst of all on her bed. The walls were light brown and wet-looking, like caramel, from years of chain-smoking. There were inches of dust on tables. There was no door on her bathroom. I can't remember how it came off and more important why it was never fixed. It had really been years since anything had gotten fixed, since we tried to maintain her. Which had seemed reasonable before, not "enabling" her any longer, sane even, but which now did not seem reasonable or sane. The first rule of alcoholism: You can't get anyone else sober. The second rule: If your mother dies of alcoholism in a mice-infested shithole in the West Village all alone, you're never going to feel good about it, you're never going to feel you did enough and you will definitely feel like you should have out-fucked that first rule and saved your mother's life.

There was an old-lady gismo on her toilet seat, something you see in a hospital, something you turn from, not wanting to know the names for such indignities that might await even you. There was a walker. She was sixty-four. Who knew it was going to be this awful? Did we? I mean . . . did we?

As Katharine and Julia and I stared at the squalor and in particular the mouse droppings everywhere, the buzzer sounded.

"Exterminator."

We were semi-paralyzed around the intercom. The farcical entrance of an exterminator was like the bell ringing and it being Betty Ford. We don't need you now, Betty. She's dead. Where the fuck were you ten years ago? Eight years ago? Two years ago? Shit, Betty, are you on the sauce again?

"Umm, we don't need you today. Thanks," Katharine blurted.

We looked at one another and around the apartment for some way in, some indication of where to start. "This is not going to end well," my mother would say about fifty times a day, mostly when the four of us girls were throwing one another down staircases or rigging things over doorways to fall on one another, and I can't help remembering this saying of hers, because not only did her life not end well, it didn't end badly. It ended horrifically, one of the worst endings I've ever seen to a life. And when this happens, when this happens to your mother, what do you remember? Which Mom? Which mornings? Which nights? What do you leave and what do you take with you? Clearly I'm not here looking for day-count coins from AA. But is there something here that will work for me, that will help me find I don't fucking know what? She no longer has to be or not be anything to anyone. She didn't get sober. She wasn't the mom I wanted her to be. I wanted her to fight. Fight. Fight. Fight. But she didn't, obviously. And it was over. So then why was I scanning the joint like it was my own brain: deducing the love, the anger, the confusion, looking for her, in death, to be something I could live with? We were here to clean out her apartment, to get rid of things. But it seemed I was actually here to acquire a mother.

There was a lamp that looked even too gloomy to be in a Tennessee Williams play. It was a standing lamp with a table around the middle like a child's water float. It had a big ivory-colored lampshade, browned by wear, and it had a bad tear in the middle of the shade. The top half of the lamp was stooped over to one side in misery. It could go no further. Katharine and Julia and I stared at it. I felt awful for this lamp. Going through various papers and legal documents around her apartment, we found insurance photos of my mother's father, Grampe's house on Litzsinger Road in Ladue, St. Louis. I spotted the lamp in one. You could see it in its heyday—polished regularly, upright, shining with dignity. This lamp didn't deserve this.

After about fifteen years and ten rehabs and detoxes, my sisters and I had decided we couldn't help her. Her dog walker took over for a while, until the day he found my mother under a desk with the D.T.'s when he returned from walking Emma. Assorted therapists kept her alive, and West Village boys helped her get by, like her drinky pal Marcel, until she accused him of stealing her Xanax. Then various people from the Perry Street group of AA helped, until it became clear she didn't want a virgin mojito any more than she wanted to "go gray," and at that point it was my father who became her final caretaker.

Anyone who came near her got caught in her lair of need. A new neighbor, a delivery boy, my brand-new boyfriend might find themselves receiving late-night phone calls about Rodney, the boy she should have married, God damn it, or running to the corner to get her a carton of True Blues, tending to her endless groany requests until they became a resentment factory who hated themselves for the way they were treating someone so obviously petite. Like Montgomery Clift in *A Place in the Sun.* He's in love with Elizabeth Taylor, but he's gotten Shelley Winters pregnant already, and her maddening neediness turns him into a murderer essentially. My mother was not just about who she became, she was about who she made you become.

She got around an awful lot by ambulance at this point in her life, but if she had to go anywhere other than the emergency room at St. Vincent's, someone had to take her. Occasionally I took her to doctors' appointments on the condition that we "stop by" an AA meeting on the way home. I tried to call her at least once a week but admittedly saw her as little as possible. I found her apartment very difficult—when I did go there I would be depressed for weeks afterward.

I wanted to be a better daughter than I was. If I couldn't cure her I should have been her unflappable nurse. I would like nothing more than to recount tales of how I regularly went over, made her soup just to have in the fridge, brought her unauthorized biographies of Lady Di, watched Lifetime with her at three in the morning. I wish I could say I did all these things when my mother became the kind of drinker who wakes up and doesn't know if it's five in the morning or five in the afternoon, I wish I could tell myself that I did all I could. But I don't think I can.

After about age forty-eight, she claimed to not be able to walk anywhere, not even down a flight of stairs to a cab, which was just incredibly hard to believe. The Thanksgiving before she died, Katharine was cooking dinner at her new house and my mother was making a big stink about making the trip.

"Windsor Terrace? Who ever heard of . . . Windsor Terrace? It all sounds awful. I just don't know what to do."

"Get in a cab, Mother," I suggested.

"A cab? A cab will take me to Windsor Terrace?"

"Yes, Mother."

"I'm not sure you're right about that one, sweet pea."

"I swear, Mom. Just tell them the address."

"Cabs don't like to go to Brooklyn, Jeanne. Did you know that?"

"Well, they have to, Mom. It's the law."

"What if he leaves me on the Brooklyn Bridge? Oh, this is insanity. Absolute insanity."

"I'll borrow Kate's car and drive you home if you take a cab there."

"It sounds like a royal pain in the ass. Brooklyn is a real pain in the ass in my opinion."

Silence.

"Will you tell Kate and Henry that I'm so sorry Mom's such a burden that they couldn't come pick me up? Tell them I understand what a difficult meal Thanksgiving is to put together, what with the peas and mashed potatoes and cranberry sauce. It's not like they're making pot-au-feu for twenty-five, which is what I did with you girls. I had huge dinner parties and four babies, not one, and an enormous house to take care of."

"Can you just get in a cab? Geez. Why do you have to be so difficult?"

"Oh, now I'm the difficult one?"

"You've always been the difficult one!"

"I have had just about enough. I don't have to listen to one more minute of this—"

She hung up. My phone rang a minute later.

"Hello?"

"It's Mother. I wanted to let you know I just put in a call to Bill Shames, my lawyer in St. Louis, because I am going to SUE YOU for everything you've got, which I realize, hah, isn't much."

"You're suing me?"

"That's right, baby."

"For what?"

"For acting like an insensitive maniac."

"You're suing me for acting like an insensitive maniac?"

"That's right. You'll be hearing from my attorney, dearie."

I should have picked her up.

———————

There was blood on her couch from the day she had the stroke. My father called me the day before we were to go clean my mother's apartment.

"Now, Jean-Joe, should I go over to Mama's and take the bloody couch out of view so that you girls don't have to be traumatized by seeing that? Is seeing that awful blood on Mama's couch going to be . . . uh, traumatizing, do you think? Although where in the hell am I going to drag a bloody couch to . . . I'll probably get arrested . . . I suppose I could just throw a blanket over the bloodstains on the couch so you wouldn't have to see all that blood. I could always do that." It would simply never occur to my father that perhaps repeating the words "bloody," "Mama," "stains," and "couch" in various combinations might have taken care of whatever traumatizing remained to be done.

We divvied up the jobs at the beginning of each day there, and today I was on clothes. I wondered whether I would find any Lenox Hill Hospital robes. Lenox Hill Hospital on the Upper East Side used to have these really chic robes—blue-and-white seersucker, shortish. My mother was a regular there when she lived on East Eighty-seventh Street, and my sisters and I couldn't get enough of them. The problem was that our friends also took a shine to these bad boys, and before you knew it we were fielding requests from all over town.

"Jean, hey, it's Sophia. I don't want to be insensitive, but if your mom goes to detox again in the near future, could you nab me a medium?"

I didn't find any of the robes. I put things in bags that would go in the garbage. I didn't want to give any of it to Goodwill, because I am a serious thrifter and I was horrified at the idea of coming across any of my mother's things in a secondhand store. Though from the apartment I was the only one of us who took anything wearable, anything that required putting a piece of my mother's smell anywhere near me. Nothing could compete with the way my mother smelled at the end. The cigarettes, the old vodka smell mixed with the new vodka smell, the greasy hair, the hundred-dollar-an-ounce Parisian stench called Joy. I think Kate sent my mother's jewelry to the dry cleaners. Figuring I could wash things a few hundred times, I took one totally queer yellow-and-navy-blue-striped boat-neck shirt from L.L.Bean, one fantastic Indian-print muumuu from the '60s, a cream-colored cashmere sweater from L.L.Bean, one navy-blue wool jacket that my dad gave her from Brooks Brothers. She had never even been on the Internet, so L.L.Bean catalogs became her only option for clothes, her one-stop shut-in shop. I don't know why I took these clothes, because they were not clothes that represented her particularly.

Later that day while Julia worked on the kitchen, I transferred myself from closets to the bookshelves, which were loaded with crap. My mother didn't have affairs, she read commercial fiction to make my father insane. There was also the matter of her tendency when she went to rehab to stash money in books, so each book had to be gone through before being sent to Goodwill. It was genetic; her mother, not a drinker, was also a cash stasher, although my grandmother stashed cash in her refrigerator crisper drawer.

There were the expected hits on my mother's shelves: the Big Book of Alcoholics Anonymous, *How to Quit Drinking Without AA, Sober for Good, Seven Weeks to Sobriety, The Neutral Spirit: A Portrait of Alcohol* by friend Berton Roueché. The recovery section also contained the *Social Register*—we were kicked out in the late '80s because we never bought the black-and-orange books put out every year. Going through her books reminded me of the book my mother had given her new granddaughter, Louisa, several years before.

After seeing Louisa for the first time my mother had headed out to Kate's deck to have a cig. Katharine went and put Louisa down for a nap. Coming back inside, Mom announced that she had a present for the baby. Katharine and Mom sat on the couch with Mom rummaging through her bag madly, finally finding the item and pulling it out of her bag and holding it out to Katharine. It was unwrapped. A book traveled from Mom's to Kate's hands and Katharine read the title.

"*Hannibal* by Thomas Harris."

"Mmm hmm."

"*Hannibal*. Like Hannibal the cannibal? *Silence of the Lambs*? Anthony Hopkins's character who eats people with fava beans?" Kate asked.

"Right. Did you read the first one?" Mom asked.

"Um, well, no. This is—"

"It's for the baby," Mom said.

"Right. For the baby. She's two months old."

"I know, sweetie, you're going to have to read it to her."

"Right. Thanks, Mom."

"You're welcome. It's really terrific."

"Yeah. Well, she definitely doesn't have it."

Henry came in the door from work.

"Hi, Doris."

"Hello, Henry. The baby's beautiful, just beautiful."

"Aw, thanks, Doris."

"I have to go. I just came to bring the baby a present." Mom got up.

Henry put his bag down on the couch. Kate held up the book.

"*Hannibal*," Henry read, looking like someone had struck him between the eyes with a park bench. "Like Hannibal the cannibal?"

"Yeah." Kate glared at him. Henry got up and went to the phone.

"Thanks so much, Doris. Here, let me call the car. I know the fastest one."

On the shelf below all the how-to-quit-drinking books was a photo album of my mother's debutante party, the Fleur de Lis Ball. It was like a wedding album, a professional book of about fifty or so photographs of the party at her house. Everything was so displayed back then. People. Soup. Gifts. Cigarettes. I stared at a picture of a long table where presents were displayed with my mother posed in front of it, while behind me Julia took a piss in the bathroom with no door.

Kate and Julia began boxing up the endless parade of silver: silver brushes, rulers, letter openers, trophies from horse shows, platters, picture frames, bowls, trivets, trays, cigarette boxes, cigarette cases, flasks, decanters. All of it engraved. Engravers must have been busier than McCarthy in the '50s. Ditto for monogrammers. The number of monogrammed linens that my mother had was preposterous. I agreed to take three gigantic boxes of fancy schnoz-blowers, and it is not lost on me that I have inherited a lifetime supply of hankies from the world's weepiest mother.

"Eek!" Kate screamed and then started huffing immediately. Julia and I rushed over to where she was going through a pile of family photo albums and giant framed portraits.

"What? Mouse?" Julia asked.

"Stay back!" Kate yelped. We froze in our places. "There was this grungy old piece of pink tissue paper stuck in this crappy old photo album from Amagansett and when I barely touched it diamonds came tumbling out and now they're everywhere!"

"Fuck," I said, not being a diamond lover so much as just someone who can relate to spilling shit.

"They're really small, they're not big like a ring or Mom's diamond earrings. They're teeny little diamonds."

"Like diamond flakes?" Julia asked, putting on her glasses.

"No." Kate tried desperately to remain calm. "What are

diamond flakes? No, they're diamonds. I'm just saying, there's a lot of them and they're very small and this place is a disaster so be really careful moving stuff around."

We began searching. Kate started with her cleavage, which was a smart move, as stuff does tend to land there: contacts, food, earrings. I bent down to examine the area around Kate's feet. Julia started with the perimeter behind Kate, presumably looking for any diamonds that had jumped out of the coke bindle they were wrapped in and powered themselves off Kate's pregnant belly up and backward, behind her right shoulder.

"Here's some!" I said triumphantly and picked up three little diamonds. "Where are we putting these?" I asked, looking up at Kate.

"Um, I say we put them in this little jewelry pouch over here."

I handed her the diamonds and kept looking. "Move your feet," I told Kate, and she lifted one foot and held it up for me to look under and then lifted the other and held it as long as she could.

Julia must have thought we were working on commission because she came around to where I had found my diamonds and started searching there, sort of pushing me out of my sales territory. I stood up and began looking on the edge of a destroyed armchair. It had tattered arms from my mother dropping lit cigarettes on it, and big stains on its seat. I gently moved my hand back and forth over the ratty, burnt arms looking for a girl's best friend.

Julia found six more diamonds in the carpeting and Kate

found one single diamond still in the coke bindle tissue paper. At that point we decided to have lunch.

After lunch I resumed my work at the bookshelves. The diamonds somehow reinforced what I had been thinking when I had assigned myself to the bookshelves, that Mom put things in strange places, places she was in no condition to ever find again, and I wanted to make sure that the three of us found everything. The thing is, the three of us weren't looking for the same things. I was still looking for something very specific, though I didn't know where or what it was. I wasn't going to leave this dump without my mother, whatever she was.

I had wanted her to die. In that way, the final phone call was what I had been hoping for. It's over. She's dead. She's finally dead. It was of course shocking that my mother was dead, but the second thought was, My God, what took so long? The woman survived two decades of what Nicolas Cage could endure only a single long weekend of in Vegas. My mother was Leaving Ladue, Leaving East Hampton, Leaving Bronxville, Leaving Naples, Leaving the Upper East Side, and finally Leaving the West Village. Wishing Mom was dead had been a desire for sense. Here was a person who should be dead. She had eluded the most serious of conditions, overdoses, falls, accidents, small fires. Death was the thing that would make sense. Wishing she would go was also a desire to feel loved by her. If she died, then I would have had a mother who loved me but just happened to be dead. If she continued living, then I had a mother who was killing herself slowly while I did nothing. This must have been a very different experience for Katharine and Eleanor and Julia, because they're not alcoholic. They probably felt bewildered at how this could happen to someone. As an alcoholic myself, I know exactly how this can happen, and furthermore I know this could happen to me.

As I flipped through a Julia Child cookbook, I spotted a recipe in Mom's handwriting for frozen rum raisin ice cream. It was written in pencil on the back of a card from the Oak Hill School. There was an oak leaf on it and it said OAK HILL SCHOOL at the top and then read: "This is to certify that . . . Jeanne Darst . . . has been recognized for . . . outstanding work and cooperation in French class. Date . . . October 1973." I think I've turned out fairly decently, considering I was learning French at four years old in St. Louis. On the back is the recipe for frozen rum raisin ice cream:

Finely chop ½ cup raisins and soak in ½ cup dark rum for an hour. Whip 1 cup heavy cream and fold in rum raisin mixture, ½ cup macaroon crumbs and ½ cup chopped walnuts. Gradually stir mixture into vanilla ice cream and spoon into 6 dessert dishes and freeze. Garnish and top with chopped walnuts.

I felt so lucky I wanted to scream out like Kate had done, but it was not that kind of score. For me, it was her. She was disorganized, a school report card would do just as well as anything for a recipe, she wasn't a precious homemaker, she liked to eat in the kitchen at the big butcher-block table unless she made something complicated and wanted a dining room to honor the dish. Her handwriting looked like the handwriting of every other Catholic girl turned housewife from that period, very neat, slightly rounded cursive. Was she saving a great recipe for rum raisin ice cream or my report card from preschool? Knowing her, probably both.

I wanted things that would help me remember her ordinariness, not her debutante ball or her fancy upbringing or her physical beauty or her equestrian achievements or her sultry movie star voice. Somewhere between her swanky childhood in St. Louis and her tragic death, my mother was ordinary. Cooking, sitting around the kitchen, figuring out what to have for dinner and smoking was her favorite kind of day. It was her best time. I felt this when I read the handwritten rum raisin ice cream recipe. This was what mattered. This was what I decided to take with me. It felt like I couldn't get any closer to her than this thing that she had written, a piece of her handwriting.

She was a mother, and in being that, she loved me, and I loved her. I stuffed it into my bag and went back to the bookshelves.

MANIFEST PREGNANCY

I LEANED OUT the third-floor window of a five-story town house on East Seventy-third Street off Madison. I had come to wrangle the hydrangeas. The week before, I had planted these hydrangeas in the window boxes, and then my boss got a call from the lady of the house saying her hydrangeas were sagging; this wasn't metaphor but actual saggy hydrangeas, the tops leaning over onto Seventy-third Street as if they were about to take their own lives.

Dirk, the owner of City Gardens, picked up all his workers at the Bergen Street 2/3 subway station in Brooklyn around seven a.m. and gave us all rides to our various locations for the day. Most of his workers were sober and most were men, but Dirk hired me for the same reason he hired the guys who worked for him: I was clearly someone who couldn't get or keep her shit together and no one else would hire me. I rode in the back of the van, sitting on bags of mulch with all the guys I knew from the sobriety circuit. There was always a day where someone didn't have money for lunch, and today it was me. This guy Mike gave me five bucks. I found a banana someone had left on a flat of liriope, and it was unharmed, so I thought I'd just have that and a bag of almonds I brought from home for lunch and save the five bucks Mike gave me for an emergency.

"Okay, Jeanne, you're working alone at the Fenners'," Dirk said, pulling over.

I hated working alone, and I didn't love this particular house. The house manager always yelled at me for tracking dirt on the carpets, and the young hot Polish nanny made me sad—her life looked so lonely.

I was using little sticks and string to prop up the suicidal hydrangeas. There were five floors, three windows per floor, and about four hydrangeas in each box. I had been doing this shit for hours. Marianne, the tall, fit black woman who ran the house, appeared in the doorway, startling me.

"You left your muddy boots next to the door. Carol saw them first thing when she walked in."

"Sorry. Who's Carol?"

"The woman who owns this place and is about to come in here and get all Medea on you," Marianne snapped. Marianne could be made to be fun; it was just a lot of work. We often watched *All My Children* when no one was around.

"Well, Medea killed her own children, not the gardeners, so perhaps you should alert the kids upstairs." I looked at my watch. "Shit. I gotta go. I gotta catch a plane." I jumped up and collected my trowels and sticks and the clear plastic sheeting that had to be put over everything.

"You better get one of those other drug addicts to finish this window."

"Recovering. Recovering drug addicts," I said, folding the sheeting and putting it in my big bag.

"Oh, right! Recovering. Well, it seems more like resting if you ask me. Taking a break. Resting drug addicts. They always go back."

"Not always. Three percent of us never use again!"

"Oh, excuse me!" Marianne said.

Heading toward the subway, I decided I needed a slice. Landscaping was the most physically exhausting work I had ever done, which was not entirely a point of woman-pride. It felt pretty stupid most days. What was I trying to prove? Why didn't I just get a regular job? How long could I do this?

I got in line at the pizza place, getting out the five Mike had given me, waiting for the owner of the place to get to me.

There is definitely a difference between working shit jobs when you're in your twenties and all your friends are working shit jobs, too, and working shit jobs when everyone except you has decided to fuck being an actress and has gone to law school and/or gotten married, is having kids and wearing comfortable clothing while you're still "doing your thing." I was headed to Palm Beach to do *Sally on the Mount* at my friend's boyfriend's house. I was going from being the gardener at a fancy New York town house to being the talent at a house show in Palm Beach. It was an upgrade, definitely, but I wasn't sure why I was doing it other than for the money, which was reason enough. I thought it made sense. I couldn't tell anymore.

The pizza guy repeated something he'd said while I was spacing out.

"What can I get you, sir?"

Sir? Sir? I was now a sir? I now looked so hideous, so dirt-covered and disheveled and ugly that people thought I was a man? I was paralyzed. He must have needed glasses, or would realize his mistake momentarily. He continued looking right at me. "Sir?"

Fuck it. What was I going to do? "One plain." Shit. I took my slice and left, eating while I walked to the number 6 train at Seventy-seventh Street.

AT HOME I TOOK OFF my Carhartts and my City Gardens sweatshirt and jumped in the shower. My boyfriend of five months, Nick, called to see how I was doing. Nick used to have a junk shop on Fifth Avenue in Park Slope. Katharine and I would go and check him out occasionally on the weekends. He got married and moved to L.A., but he'd come back to Brooklyn occasionally. One day I ran into him on the street, and he told me he was getting divorced.

"I'm so sorry," I said, having no idea whether my face was matching my words.

And then a couple months later we were dating. I've always felt that the ideal way to live is to go to bed with someone and wake up alone. Heaven. But Nick had a quality that I hadn't found in guys for about a decade: he didn't drive me insane. I was doing my show in L.A., staying at his house, when my mom died. Nick's dad had died only about a year earlier. His father, unlike my mother, died suddenly. He was struck by lightning while out for a run in the rain in Tampa, Florida, which, according to Nick, is the lightning-striking-and-killing-you capital of the United States.

"Are you okay?" Nick asked.

"I feel okay, but some guy just called me 'sir,' so maybe I don't look so great. I was a little nauseous earlier, but I think it was this banana I found in Dirk's truck. Maybe it was bad."

"A bad banana? Not likely. Stop eating food you find in Dirk's truck, baby. You're probably pregnant."

"Ha! Yeah."

"You are, I bet."

"Stop it, Jesus."

"It'd be great. I love you. I love our baby—"

"STOP!" I laughed.

"Go run to the corner and get an EPT."

"I don't need to do one of those."

After getting off the phone, I realized I did need to take an EPT. If only because he had now made me anxious. And maybe excited. I threw on some sweatpants and went to buy a test. I got home and did it immediately. It said I was pregnant. I took another one and it said "ditto." I called Nick.

"I'm pregnant."

"I told you!" he yelled. He was happy. I was happy. We were happily pregnant. He was meeting me in Florida the following day.

When I got off the plane in Palm Beach, my old friend Cassie was standing outside the terminal smoking a cigarette, talking on her BlackBerry.

She hung up and screamed, "AHHHH! What's up, nigga?"

A black man got out of a car in front of her.

We headed to some swanky spot in town for lunch. The whole weekend was their treat, and I was also getting paid nicely. The menu was filled with dishes—aged carpaccio, pork loin salad, whole roasted Chilean sea bass on a bed of fennel—I hadn't eaten since before the War on Terror. Cassie told me about some recent trips she and Harry, her boyfriend, had taken.

"You would have loved Croatia, Jeanne. We had to refuel there after Russia, so we hopped out for a few days. The Croatian people are incredible."

I couldn't imagine whom they could possibly have been hanging out with. Did they rent a Croatian couple for the long weekend? Lately, before seeing her, I had started prepping myself with an ancient Buddhist mantra: She can't help it. She can't help it. She can't help it.

I looked at her diamond studs, Cartier watch and Mafia-wife handbag. I could live for six months on her dry-cleaning bill alone. Raskolnikov would have clubbed her over the head with his whole roasted Chilean sea bass already.

"This is so cool! I'm so glad you decided to come," she said.

I looked around the restaurant at the Palm Beach women:

lots of plastic surgery, Lilly Pulitzer–covered wheelchairs, blond toddlers in navy blazers.

"Do you think Harry is going to like my show?" I asked.

"Harry loves your show," she said.

"He hasn't seen it yet," I said.

"You know what I mean," she said.

My room was above some kind of billiards-in-Africa-themed room with a giant bar. There were stuffed animals, photo albums from safaris her boyfriend had been on, leather club chairs.

My quarters were gigantic and had a view of the water and looked down on the patio. There was a big telescope in my room, but I couldn't figure out how to use it. I was eager for Nick to get here. I went to sleep wondering what it was going to be like to see him now that we were a family. I barely knew Nick at this point. I mean, yes, we were in love but we'd been dating only for five months and on different coasts. This was how I did everything. How I wrote everything. By instinct, without thinking. One day I'm trying to avoid cat shit while planting shrubs outside a housing development in Crown Heights, the next I'm deciding I'm ready to be a mother?

The next morning from my window, I spied Cassie on the patio so I made my way down.

"Is your room okay?" she asked.

"It'll do." I smiled. "I'm pregnant," I said.

"What?"

"Yeah. I know."

"Holy shit, Jeanne. You're going to be a mom."

"Okay, okay, let's not get dramatic." Like when I quit my job at Sundance and my therapist let out a squeal of horror, I hated when people had big reactions to my life. It made me feel like my impulsiveness and running my life on instinct (Am I brave or stupid?), the things I worried about in myself, weren't exactly going unnoticed. "What are you doing, you broke-ass, disorganized lunatic?" was what it felt like they were saying.

Nick came in from L.A. that night. He was going to film the show and, as it turned out, have a lot of fun filming me throwing up and moaning in bed. When we hugged at the airport, it was sudden and strange and shocking how much things had changed, and also how much I was okay with it. We could do this. I could be a writer *and* be in a relationship *and* have a child. Writing did not require a solo life, and artists did not have to be shit-faces.

Back at the house, Nick and I lay around, me drinking ginger ale for my nausea, trying to figure out if it was possible that I got pregnant the week my mom died. Maybe the same day? Nick seemed to get who I was, what I liked to do with my time—mainly spend copious amounts of it alone writing plays and then putting them on and wearing costumes and having some laughs with my friends afterward. He seemed to understand this about me. He had a lot of his own things going on, too, which comforted me. He was a painter who ran his own art galleries and did the occasional real estate flipping. A life together seemed viable and exciting.

The show was happening the Saturday night before Easter Sunday in Palm Beach. The weird factor was sky high. Formal invitations had been sent out. There were one hundred and fifty guests expected for drinks around the pool, then dinner for a hundred and fifty on the patio. Caterers were running around setting up. There was valet parking, a stage had been built, gardeners were hanging extra vines on the house to make it look nice, a piano was brought out to the white tent–covered performance area, there was a lighting person, a piano tuner, and a DJ for dancing after my show. This was a show that began in my living room in Brooklyn as a way to raise my rent money.

I got out of my sick bed about twenty minutes before showtime and put on my fishnets, high-heeled gladiator boots, bustier. I tailored the open to the setting, wearing a crazy Palm Beach hat and Lilly Pulitzer hot pants, making jokes about tax day and Easter. All the tanned oldies in their blue blazers and penny loafers were with me, really laughing, but after the open I noticed people were making repeated trips to the bar and getting quiet, aka drunk-sleepy. By about halfway through, a third of the audience was asleep. I could have given a shit, really. I wanted the chance to perform my show for a demographic that simply was not going to find me at an experimental jazz club on the Lower East Side. So what if half of them didn't get the jokes or fell asleep? It was unusual and house theater, which I loved, and most important I got $3,500 for doing my show for one night. I could live on $3,500 for two months in Brooklyn and it made me feel like maybe I could make money as a writer.

The next day we headed to the airport. Nick had to go back to L.A. and I was going with him. We didn't talk extensively about where we would live. He owned a house in Los Angeles. I had a landscaping job in Brooklyn. I wasn't going to win this one. As we were waiting for the plane to take off I thought about how my mother left the world so slowly, so achingly, with many false starts, much suffering for herself and my dad and my three sisters. And here was this kid who popped into the world as easily as my mother had left painfully. I am getting on a plane to go to Los Angeles and have a baby, I told myself, as if it was simply my next gig. I could do that.

Right after we got to Los Angeles, I began vomiting out our car window, into a bucket by our bed, next to taco trucks while Nick got a couple *al pastor*. Then, as I gripped the plastic blue bucket that now rested at my side like a pug in a Goya painting, it hit me: I live in L.A. I vomited several more times. It seemed like in order to grasp the fact that I was pregnant I had to first figure out where the hell I was. I called my friends in Brooklyn. They confirmed my theory.

"You live in L.A."

"Yes, my pal, you live in L. fuckin' A."

Nick drove everywhere for the first trimester, partly because I was liable to get sick but also because I felt that if I didn't drive, then I wasn't really there. And if I never figured out where anything was or how to get anywhere, we'd just have to move back to New York where I could be pregnant along with Katharine, who was four months pregnant with her second child. She was due in August, I was due in December. After I'd been there for a few weeks I figured it was time to call Dad and tell him I was pregnant before Katharine or Eleanor let it slip.

"Hi, Dad. It's Jean. Yes, I'm still out in California. Nick and I have some news. I'm pregnant."

"And getting married?" he asked.

"Yes," I said.

Nick and I had talked about getting married and he wasn't that excited about the idea, he hadn't been divorced that long, but I wanted to get married, which surprised me. It's not that I had always thought marriage itself was bad, what I thought was that marrying the wrong person was bad, really bad. That's what will leave you wanting to jump off a chaise longue to your death. And I thought that if you had a lot of kids, I don't know, more than two maybe, that you could go insane just taking care of them, especially if you never had any money for an occasional babysitter or something. But other than going insane or being suicidal, I thought marriage and kids was probably a good thing. I didn't want to get married because I was worried anyone in my family might think it was important, which my dad definitely did. I wanted it spontaneously, after the nausea cleared, because I wanted to tell everyone I knew the good news, to celebrate. Mom's death was about large, complicated emotions, with grim specifics, and no one in the family wanted to do anything public. Which I understood. But, the way I saw it, my last family had just ended so sadly, and if Nick and I were truly happy about this family, which we were, why would I want to be discreet about it?

Trying to love L.A., as Nick and Randy Newman did, wasn't going as well. At a movie, a man in the aisle in front of me was eating not popcorn I noticed, but a bag of raw spinach. And unlike everyone else, I was just not that impressed with sunshine. It was okay, it was fine, yes, of course it was lovely at the right time. But blazing, nonstop, meaningless sun that washed out everything wasn't beautiful to me and I couldn't get away from it. Sometimes I just got so mad at the sun I yelled, which made me look insane. Nick didn't understand why I was so incensed that it was sunny all the time.

"Well, you must miss your friends but you can't beat the weather!" a stranger said to me at a coffee shop.

"Yeah, I guess." And then I said it. "I don't love it, the weather."

I got that look, the one that said, Wow, you're so . . . toxic or negative or angry. Like that was a bad thing.

In my mind, L.A. was not a place to grieve. It was just too sunny. You can't mourn your mother in eyeball-scorching sunshine. Also, when you're trying to feel the end of someone, it's appalling to be sitting next to fifty-year-olds in coffee shops who are wearing pink Vans sneakers and red skinny jeans and T-shirts that say things like "You Can't Make Me."

I was so used to people in New York asking, "What do you do?" that when people in Los Angeles would look at my pregnant belly and ask, "When are you due?" I would reflexively answer, "I'm a writer." I discovered people in L.A. don't want to be judged by what they do. People here are all human beings, not "human doings." Turns out I liked human doings better.

I couldn't grasp that real writers live in Los Angeles. I actually called my old writing teacher and asked, "Do you think I could write a book in L.A.?" And he said, "People have done it, you know."

Moving across the country, for all my derring-do onstage and in life, was totally against my character. I was a New Yorker, and if you are a real New Yorker, you don't leave. You want to leave all the time but you don't. That's something fake New Yorkers do. The same way that if you're really part of a family, you don't leave it. To leave the family physically felt more drastic. Like leaving a self behind. What getting sober felt like. Not that I planned on being a Californian. But I did have to get rid of my tear-jerkingly cheap Park Slope share.

On a quick trip back East to pack up my old apartment I told Nick I needed more time to box things up and that he should go back to L.A. and I'd meet him back there in a day or so. He looked at me and said, "I'm not going back to L.A. without you." The mixture of devotion and mistrust was touching. He got me. He knew I loved him and our unborn child. He also knew how much I loved the hot-and-sour soup at the corner of Sixth and Union.

I insisted that we spend the last trimester in New York, where we would get married and I would give birth a month later, otherwise who the hell was going to visit me in the hospital afterward? Nick complied and we crowded into the Brooklyn apartment with our subletter. I bought the 1971 embryology sleeper *From Conception to Birth: The Drama of Life's Beginnings* at one of my favorite secondhand bookstores, Heights Books on Montague Street. According to the authors, intelligence and personality emerge in the third trimester, a time I had now ensured we would be spending in New York. Who was disorganized pregnant lady now?

The wedding was on a barge in Red Hook, Brooklyn, in my eighth month. As my dad began walking me down the aisle, or "the plank" as he called it because it was again, a barge dock, the *QE2* began pulling out of the harbor. I made him stop and wait for the ship to pass, because otherwise I was going to be this preggo bride with an ocean liner behind me and that was too disturbing an image to have in my memory. I was gigantic, having miscalculated how pregnant I was going to be, thinking seven months but I was actually eight months pregnant. My friend Cassie had loaned me the most outrageous high shoes to wear with my silver sequin dress. I could definitely have swung them. Nick was not happy about me walking in high shoes at eight months pregnant, and the day before the wedding he forced me to go to Aerosoles, the comfortable-shoe store, and get some two-inch numbers that someone's grandmother might wear. I ended up writing a poem to read during the ceremony about going to Aerosoles with him, about how he was, certainly, the more practical of the two of us and that our differences were what made us us.

So while we waited for the QE2 to pass, Dad talked about Kennedy's inauguration day. He also let me know he was "flying on prednisone," his steroid medication for his asthma. The next day, many of my friends let me know that my dad had told them he was "flying on prednisone" as well.

We had just a few weeks as married people before the baby was due. My due date was December 7, Mom's fake birthday. December 7 came and went, no baby. Then her real birthday, December 11, passed, no baby. I was somewhat relieved these two dates were not my baby's birthday. On December 15, my son was born. In less than a year my mother had died, I had gotten pregnant, gotten married, moved to Los Angeles, and had a baby.

Four weeks later, we were getting ready to go back to Los Angeles. Nick checked our tickets to verify the departure time the next day and came running into the room where I was nursing and yelled, "It's today! Our flight is today not tomorrow. Today! In three hours! Come on! Let's go! Let's go! Let's go!!!!!"

I was running around, throwing diapers in bags and clothes in bags, when my dad called. This is the kind of phone call that the second you pick up the phone your whole body says, WHAT THE FUCK DID YOU DO THAT FOR? THAT WAS THE WORST DECISION YOU HAVE EVER MADE! YOU'RE CRAZY! YOU'VE ALWAYS BEEN CRAZY!

"Jean-Joe, how goes it?"

"Not good, actually, I can't talk."

"I'm in your neighborhood."

"Oh. Um, well, we thought we were leaving tomorrow but it's today. Like right now." I was opening the fridge and chucking Chinese food containers in the garbage.

"I'll just drop in and see you off."

"Oh, gosh, I don't know, Dad. We have to get this whole operation to JFK in about forty minutes."

"I'm at the bookstore across the street."

"Dad, I uh . . ."

"Well, I've gotta give Hudson this present I got him."

OH! Present, well, why didn't you say so? Come on over.

We hung up and he buzzed our buzzer in under two minutes. He followed me back to the kitchen where he handed me a brown paper bag. The present.

"Did you know Murray's cheese shop was closing? Well, I ran right over there, Jean-Joe—my God, was I in shock. Turns out they're just moving across the street."

I opened the bag, and there, in some waxed paper, was a hunk of blue cheese.

"Damn good blue there I got for Huddie. Stilton, I believe."

I looked up at my dad. "Well, Dad, he can't, uh, he's only, you know, four weeks."

"Well, if you think he doesn't want it—" he said, as if my son were particular.

"It's not that he doesn't want it—he's not a snob or something, Dad, he's a newborn."

"It's a soft cheese," he said, taking a bite of the cracker he made for himself.

"No, I know . . ."

"Let's have at it ourselves, shall we?" He plunked some on a cracker and handed it to me. I took it appreciatively and when he turned his back to make another one for himself, I threw it in the freezer. It was ten-forty a.m. I wasn't eating blue cheese before noon, I didn't care if Murray's was relocating to the Gaza Strip. I was still hobbling around from my hatchet job of an emergency C-section, hoping my gut didn't bust open after lifting suitcases and putting stuff into them.

"Tell me, did you get a chance to look at that photocopy I made you of that essay on structural metaphors in Fitzgerald's short fiction? I know you've been busy." I told him no, not quite, been kinda swamped and stuff but I would definitely get to it.

"What are you reading lately?" he asked, and I paused, shutting the fridge door, picturing the copy of *The Happiest Baby on the Block* on my nightstand.

"Um, you know, just some, um, Joyce. *Dubliners*."

I knew this would make him happy and I wouldn't be seeing him for a while so what the hell, I thought, as he lit up. "Oh, really? Terrific! Now, tell me, have you read it before? I thought you were just lukewarm on Joyce . . ." he said, beginning a Joyce monologue that would require only head nods and umm-hmms from me for the next twenty minutes.

He gave me a photocopy of Hudson's namesake, Captain Thomas Hudson's, honorable discharge notice from the

Mexican-American War. He promised to send other historical documents as he digs them up at his house. He gave me a hug and shook Nick's hand and left. We raced around and somehow made it to the airport and made our flight, but I was a little worried that this episode might be representative of our new life. Getting married and having a baby had done nothing to make me into a calm, organized adult. My dad was never going to be the comforting, elder statesman grandfather. Was this my destiny? I didn't know. But I was going west (again) and I had definitely expanded.

MY FATHER'S OB-GYN

MY FATHER, despite being a single, nonexpecting, sexually inactive seventy-eight-year-old man, has an ob-gyn. He gets a kick out of saying, in the presence of his daughters, things like "Well, my ob-gyn says it's fine to eat the occasional piece of bacon after the first trimester." He was referred by his internist to this obstetrician-gynecologist, Dr. Carl Wallace, a man who apparently shares a love of books with my dad. Lately, with the help of his man Dr. Wallace, he's zeroed in on a hot little piece of information about Zelda Fitzgerald's obstetric history.

After her second baby, Katharine struggled in her hospital bed to get her new daughter to latch on to her breast while my father sat in the chair to her left, talking animatedly about his new finding: "Turns out the doctor was a man named Lakin. Dr. Lakin apparently performed Zelda's abortion at the Plaza Hotel in 1922. Now, plenty of biographers have known and written about this secret abortion at the Plaza, but I really think they've downplayed it, particularly in Nancy Milford's book, out of some kind of respect, which is understandable; but here's what none of them—and I mean none of my competitors—have gotten right: I believe Scott made her have this thing about four months after their daughter, Scottie, was born and it made her incapable of carrying another child to term, which mentally wrecked her. Totally. There was a fix-up job in Rome a bit later, so obviously her womb was ruined by the abortion, and Dr. Wallace says that could very easily drive a woman over the edge. Now, Katarina, let's have a look at that baby."

While Dad had been studying Fitzgerald since my adolescence, and working on a nonfiction book on him for at least ten years before my mom died, this Zelda stuff began really picking up steam after my mother died. It didn't parallel their marriage directly—I don't believe my mother had any abortions—but I wondered if it could be a symbol of the guilt my father felt for the suffering she endured as a writer's wife, as his wife. About a year after Mom died, their friend Tom Eagleton died and my father flew to St. Louis to attend his funeral. A day or so after Eagleton's funeral, Dad had my mother's ashes buried in Calvary Cemetery at the Darst family plot. When he got back it was natural to ask if he missed her. He responded as if he was a lecturer who had stumbled on his way up to the podium: "Oh, thanks for asking, Jean-Joe. Now, have I told you about my latest findings in the Fitzgerald letters at the Princeton University library?"

The Christmas when Hudson was first born, before we went back to L.A., the whole family except for Julia was at Eleanor's in Connecticut; Christmas is the only time all of us are ever together and I had wanted to take some pictures. Hudson, ten days old, was sleeping in his car seat carrier next to the tree. It was tempting to nurse a sentiment of "first Christmas with Mom gone" and "I have a brand-new baby that Mom will never know," but I caught myself, because Mom wouldn't have been here at Eleanor's house for Christmas even if she was alive, and she might not have met Hudson until he was two and a half anyway. There was some truth to those sentiments but it wasn't the full truth. Still I felt close to Eleanor and Katharine in a new way. They were happy that I hadn't missed out on being a mom and we seemed connected now as mothers, though they still made jokes about my capabilities and saw me as a die-hard spaz. At one point that night, as I finished putting a diaper on Hudson and turned my back to throw out the old one, Katharine undid the tab and refastened it.

"It was too tight," she said, looking at me as if to say, Sorry, but it was.

I wanted a memory I could keep of all this, but I couldn't find my camera, and I wandered around the house looking for it. A blind woman had lived in the house before Eleanor and her husband, and apparently there were cords running up and down the stairs and through rooms when Eleanor bought it. Whenever I was there I tried to picture a blind woman navigating a three-story, five-bedroom house using only some cord. Seems like you might just want to throw in the towel and get a ranch at a certain point if you were blind, but maybe that's just my laziness. I popped my head into the dining room, where my brother-in-law Jim and my father were still sitting at the table having a grappa, and I caught ". . . so her uterus was scraped." I yanked my head out of the room and headed into the kitchen, where Katharine and Eleanor were doing dishes.

"He's on the abortion thing again," I said.

"Yuck!" Katharine said. "Can't he give it a rest? It's Christmas, for Christ sake."

Eleanor rubbed a platter with a cloth. "Yeah, I mean, he could wait until Halloween next year, and he could tell all the kids in New Canaan his abortion stories. That'd be fun. Maybe he could work the fall fair with me this year. Actually, we need some new booths. He could work the Great American Abortions Booth."

To Dad, he's simply talking about books. He's been after Jim to represent him in negotiations with Bill Gates. He wants to contact Gates because he's heard that Gates is a big fan of Fitzgerald and *The Great Gatsby*, and that he has the last line from *The Great Gatsby* lining his library in Redmond, California. My father wants to see if he'll back putting the real Gatsby mansion, on Sands Point, in preservation. He wants Jim, a partner in a firm in New York who sees my family as a bunch of loser English majors, to broker a deal with Gates's people, who will surely want to own and preserve the real Gatsby mansion. He's constantly calling Eleanor's house asking, "Now, is Jim going to be in the office tomorrow?"

"Yes, Dad, he is."

"All right, well, let him know I'll be by tomorrow with my

dossier on Fitzgerald, and let me tell you it is going to knock Gates's socks off."

"Fine. Go by anytime."

"Say about two-thirty?"

"Anytime, Dad."

My father hasn't made it in yet to meet with his legal team, hungry young lawyers out for their first kill on a meaty literary preservation/landmark contract. He usually calls Eleanor a few days later to apologize for not stopping by the office.

"Will you give Jim my apologies? I'm coming by next Wednesday for sure. I just need to put the finishing touches on this thing." If my father ever concocts a personal fragrance, I think its name should be "Finishing Touches."

"Tell Jim I'm coming by around eleven next Wednesday without a doubt and with the goods."

A little over a year later, my father called me when I was at the playground near our house in Los Angeles. Nick was watching our son, Hudson, now fourteen months, and I was watching the two of them as my dad talked enthusiastically about Zelda's abortion for the 129th time. "It was this D-and-C, you see, that was the key to her collapse. Scott really got her into a corner about it, and she ended up having six miscarriages after it. There was another, almost criminally irresponsible, operation in Rome, allegedly to repair damages from 1922, which didn't help at all. This irreparable damage was absolutely central to her breakdown."

My cell phone was going in and out, so I couldn't hear very well, and I asked, "What was that?" My father, thinking I asked, "What *is* that?" proceeded to explain to me what an abortion is. "They take this hook-shaped metal instrument and scrape out the fetus . . ." I watched my son play in the drizzle.

"The Princeton Library has the transcript of Zelda and Scott's session with an analyst at their home in Maryland in 1933. It's about one hundred and fourteen pages and let me tell you, Jean-Joe, it'll just break your heart. I spent about three days hand-copying it there and got it down very well, I believe, verbatim, from the stenographer's record—"

I woke up. "They had a stenographer in their therapy session?" Now, that's fancy.

"That's right."

My mind jumped to the image of a stenographer getting down some of my better lines in arguments with my husband. I liked these two more and more.

"Zelda had a shorthand way of talking and of course Scott understood every word. Her mind made leaps that simply left a lot of people behind. She'd say of an attractive woman, 'She's got beautiful legs, therefore kids,' meaning, Her husband can't keep his hands off her, leading to more children. But some people didn't get her. In that way—and I don't mean in some crazy way—she was like Mama."

This was as close as I'd ever heard him come to connecting Mom to Zelda. It was unlikely he'd get any closer to what all this meant, why he was chasing the story of Zelda's demise through an abortion he felt was forced on her by her husband.

My father may feel responsible not just for my mother's life but for her actual death. He was the one who found her, and he said when she died that if he had gotten there sooner she would have survived. More to the point for me is that my alcoholic-depressive mother didn't want help, but he can't talk about that; what he can talk about is what Scott did to Zelda. When we were little he seemed to admire Fitzgerald, and then as things went bad with my mom he focused on Fitzgerald's plagiaristic ways—from Zelda, from Joyce, from Keats. Now his focus is on how Fitzgerald completely destroyed his wife through an unnecessarily dangerous abortion in 1922 at the Plaza, which he chose over a safe hospital in order to protect his reputation, as he was about to publish *The Beautiful and the Damned*. His opinion of Fitzgerald has plummeted; it feels like every time you talk to him it's gone down even further. I didn't say anything when he mentioned Mom, not that you could distinguish this silence from any previous silence in calls with him.

He sped past mentioning my mother, and the rain started coming down harder on the playground as Nick gave me the "Let's go" eyes. If it's difficult to get a word in with my father, it's Sisyphean to get off the phone with him. When you finally do manage to say "Dad? Dad. Dad!" he's already speaking your side of the conversation, saying the things that you need to say: "I know, that rain is really coming down now, you've got to go. I can hear that baby needs you, and I know I'm boring the hell out of you. Quickly, though, how's things? How's the writing?"

But there's never enough time for the present. We spend so much time in 1922 that today, the babies who are alive—his children, me, his fourteen-month-old grandson—never have a chance.

What would I tell my father if we had more than a half a second to discuss my life? It's not that he doesn't care, he does, but it's hard to reach him. He wants anecdotes to pass on to Eleanor or Katharine or Uncle Steve in St. Louis when he talks to them, he wants wit and good lines.

The truth is that I've had a baby and I want to be around my family, my sisters and my dad. I miss my friends. I don't feel I will ever like L.A. I miss walking. I miss laughing about all the things that didn't go your way that day as it seems people in New York do. I miss sarcasm. I miss talking to my friend Rosanna about a painting she's working on and then going out to her studio in Queens to see some stuff she's doing, wishing I could buy one, hinting for her to give me one, which she won't do, she can't afford to give away work. Sometimes I miss day jobs, joking around with this really funny married guy Danny at the DUMBO General Store, hearing about all the customers he'd like to but is not going to have sex with. No one here knows me, I want to tell my dad. Not even my husband. We're still getting to know each other, and the best way to get to know someone is definitely not at three in the morning when your baby won't stop crying for three hours straight and you don't know if he's sick or gassy or simply doesn't like you.

That night my father e-mailed me the document. Once Hudson was asleep, I opened the attachment on my computer. Nick came over and touched my shoulders.

"What's that?" he asked.

"It's a one-hundred-fourteen-page transcript of a therapy session between F. Scott Fitzgerald, Zelda, and their analyst in 1933 that my dad transcribed by hand. He just e-mailed it."

The hands came off my shoulders. "Whoa. Listen, I'm going to watch *The Hills Have Eyes* on my computer," Nick said, slowly backing away from me and the attachment as if we were bears. I opened it up and read it, something I planned on never doing.

STENOGRAPHER'S REPORT OF THE CONVERSATION

Between Mr. and Mrs. F. Scott Fitzgerald and DR. THOMAS A. C. RENNIE, at the Home of Mr. and Mrs. FSF, La Paix, Rodgers Forge, Towson, Maryland, Sunday, May 28, 1933, 3:30 p.m.

DR. RENNIE: Mrs. Fitzgerald, what is the paramount thing in your life: to create, or married life? I really think you will have to decide this.

(A lapse of about a minute when no one spoke.)

. . .

MR. FITZGERALD: That is the question. You see, there is an awful lot of water that has run under the bridge on your side and my side.

MRS. FITZGERALD: Dr. Rennie, I can answer that right away. I can answer that right now.

DR. RENNIE: You can answer that.

MRS. FITZGERALD: Yes. I want to write, and I am going to write; I am going to be a writer, but I am not going to do it at Scott's expense, if I can possibly avoid it. So I agree not to do anything that he does not want, a complete negation of myself, until that book is out of the way, because the thing is driving me crazy the way it is, and I cannot do that. And if he cannot adjust it, and let me do what I want to do, and live with me after that, I would rather do what I want to do. I am really sorry.

MR. FITZGERALD: In that case, would you advise a separation, Dr. Rennie?

DR. RENNIE: I would not advise anything, because I am not at all sure that Mrs. Fitzgerald knows what she wants to do. I think right now she wants to write a book. Whether she has the greatness and capacity to write great books I don't know.

MRS. FITZGERALD: That is not the point, Dr. Rennie. Something may be a sort of fulfillment of yourself, and it may not be great to other people, but it is just as essential to yourself as if it is a great masterpiece.

Fitzgerald contends that his writing is supporting them and she should not ruin their way of life with her writing. He says she is a society woman and nothing more. She feels this is what he wants her to be. He argues that she cannot write about their life because it is his material:

MR. FITZGERALD: Everything that we have done is mine. If I make a trip—I make a trip to Panama, and you and I go around—I am the professional novelist, and I am supporting you. That is all my material. None of it is your material.

. . .

DR. RENNIE: Would life for you as a creative artist compensate you for your life without Mr. Fitzgerald, if you were given the opportunity to really go on for the next twenty years and be an outstanding woman writer of this country, doing it alone? Would that mean enough when you were sixty?

MRS. FITZGERALD: Well, Dr. Rennie, I think perhaps that is a sort of a silly question.

DR. RENNIE: No, I do not think so.

MR. FITZGERALD: Why is it a silly question?

MRS. FITZGERALD: How can I tell what it would mean?

MR. FITZGERALD: Suppose I said, "I am going to sacrifice you, that is what I am going to do at any cost, I have got to develop my personality."

MRS. FITZGERALD: That is what you have said all along, and that is what you have done.

DR. RENNIE: No, he has not.

MR. FITZGERALD: Suppose I said, "I am going to sleep with every pretty woman I see, because that will make me better able to write short stories."

MRS. FITZGERALD: You have said even that to me. . . .

She basically says she'd rather be institutionalized than conventionally married:

MRS. FITZGERALD: . . . I want to be able to say, when he says something that is not so, then I want to do something so good, that I can say, "That is a God damned lie," and have something to back it up, that I can say it.

MR. FITZGERALD: Now we have found rock bottom.

DR. RENNIE: I think we have.

MRS. FITZGERALD: And I think it is better to shut yourself up in an institution than to live that way.

The thing just gets more and more interesting and zingy and, well, fun. I can understand why my father is drowning in the Fitzgeralds; they are wild and talented and fascinating. His discoveries about Zelda's gynecological history and how Scott destroyed her could be major. He's definitely onto something, I'll give him that.

When my uncle Jim died in St. Louis recently, my father's reaction was fairly stoic, which wasn't that much of a surprise; they were not on speaking terms for most of my life, but at the end, when both their wives were gone, I think they found some empathy for each other. My dad was there for Uncle Jim when Aunt Ann died, and Uncle Jim had been giving Dad some money before he died, "for the Fitzgerald project."

When my dad got back from the funeral, I called and asked him how it was, and he was perfunctory; he gave the names of the cousins who were there and who had a good line and who was sullen, and then he jumped back to the project.

"Jean-Joe, I'm off to Rockville, Maryland, this weekend to copy the diaries of a secretary of his, Laura Guthrie Hearne. He met her in Asheville, North Carolina. She was a fortune-teller who then went to Columbia and became his secretary. Oh, he paid her some miserable sum, but anyway, her diaries have a year of working for Scott in there, and I'm going to head down and photocopy the diary. Fitzgerald's downfall was he liked to drink with these people who were keeping detailed records of their time with him. My book should really be called *Don't Drink with Diarists.*"

His obsession is charming when you're talking to old friends who know him and think he is a lovable eccentric father; it's downright dangerous when you're driving to Connecticut on Christmas Eve in the freezing rain and can't roll a window down to let out some of the words that are coming at you in an endless stream, threatening to use up all available car oxygen; and it's maddening when you want him to be fucking normal for five minutes, that is, when you want him to be a person who can understand the difference between an unsavory literary obsession and conversation. Someone who can understand why you might be rankled that this topic seems more important to him than anything and anyone including his daughters, including his wife. My solo show ran about an hour, me talking for sixty minutes, but that doesn't mean I'm going to perform it without an intermission if I get you alone in a car on the Merritt Parkway.

"Who gives a shit about Zelda?" I want to shout, occasionally, when I can't take it anymore, when I miss Mom, when I can't see why she had to die just because these two couldn't seem to face up to some truths in life: that people need money to live and just might have to work from time to time and that if something like booze is killing you, you might have to give it up. Your only brother just died. Who cares about Zelda, Dad. Mom slept with mice running over her bed. And I have a son.

It can only be some kind of literary defense mechanism located in the prefrontal cortex, perhaps one that the psychiatrists and neurosurgeons have yet to discover. A part of the brain that says, "You! You, grief! You, fear! You, sadness! You, loneliness! Have you read *Tender Is the Night,* grief? Did you know that the Divers are based on my friend Honoria's father and mother, Sara and Gerald Murphy? Did you know Honoria and I were going to take a trip to Europe to find some of Gerald's lost paintings? Come over here, it's much more interesting over here, no one will find you over here, peacefully reading in this cozy part of the brain."

NOTE TO SELF

WE LOVE OUR BABY. But sometimes it seems like this might be the only thing we have. We don't see anything the same. Whenever I pull out anything of my mom's he acts like I'm trying to set the table with silverware from the *Titanic*. I think silver oyster forks and long mint julep spoons are fun, but then destruction doesn't scare me—it's part of me—whereas for him it's just too weird and frightening. I'm dragging him down. This is why he stopped painting, traded it for real estate, so he wouldn't have to live like this, and now look what I'm doing. Crazy mom! He picks at me constantly about my writing—which I'm trying to turn into a book. Working on a book—yeah, right. Killing my credit score is more like it.

When I was doing *Sally on the Mount* in Los Angeles, Marisa Tomei came to the show, and naturally she thought I was a genius and took a bunch of us out afterward to a hotel rooftop where we enjoyed seriously preferential treatment, and a large man from the hotel stood by our table for unknown reasons.

Now, a year and a half after that night with her, Nick feels, is quite insistent, that I send my book to Marisa Tomei.

"You're not even trying to get published! I don't know why you don't send that thing to Marisa Tomei."

"Well, for starters, she's not a publishing house, babe, she's an actress."

"Oh, gimme a break. You see? You don't even want to sell your book!"

"I can't . . . I just can't explain it to you, can I? Marisa Tomei is not going to publish my book."

"People don't take over two years writing a book! Why don't you send it in?"

"It's not ready."

"That's what publishers do, Jeanne. They figure out the ending. Just send it in. They'll finish it."

HUDSON AND I GO BACK to New York whenever we can, increasingly without Nick. He doesn't seem to want much to do with New York or anyone there anymore. We go out for ice cream with my dad one night. He's seventy-eight and a sub in Brooklyn public schools. He wouldn't consider teaching when we were kids, and now he's subbing in high schools. But the thing is, he really likes it. He told the black kids in school that his mother was black, telling them stories about Ella Voss, his nanny. I can't imagine what kids think of him, what they think of him saying his mother was black. I think it's hilarious but also I can't believe schools actually employ him. I ask him if Grandma Darst and Ella Voss got along. He says they did, and for the rest of the conversation refers to Grandma Darst as "your white grandmother."

He tells me he was working for the Census Bureau but he got fired because twice he was walking home at night and dropped all the papers, the data he had collected during the day. He says he retraced his steps trying to find the papers but never did. We walk to the ice cream place and sit outside on picnic benches across from Prospect Park. His front tooth is missing, fell out a few months earlier, and I can't stop staring at it. It's hard not to stare at a single jaggedy front tooth; it looks like it's protruding outward when it doesn't have another tooth next to it. It's jarring and upsetting. I have my usual mix of feelings when I see him: he's utterly delightful and likable, and he's frustrating. I am trying to figure out how I can help, does he need a social worker now, can my sisters and I pay for his expenses ourselves. My sisters are hurt mostly because his "project" still seems more important to him than their kids. As time goes on, his need to triumph becomes the only way he thinks he can redeem himself or make things right in our eyes. But as time goes on what we want more and more is a father and a grandfather. And the more he focuses on Fitzgerald the less he focuses on us and our children and the angrier Eleanor and Katharine get. I suppose they feel that he doesn't suffer for his art, they do. Their kids do. Maybe as the only one who writes, I'm more terrified for myself, and now for my son. I think, I'm next. I have just fixed two of my own teeth, albeit they were in the back so no one could see, but I was missing two teeth not six months ago. And I wonder if anyone has coined the term "writers' teeth."

He just talks through all of my thoughts, forging ahead, he's on the abortion, he's on the book, his tooth doesn't even come up. He could care less. As it has always been, his life bothers other people, not him. Hudson is psyched to see his grandpa despite his Dickensian appearance. My dad isn't sure whether he should pick his grandson up or shake his hand. He is affectionate, there is no doubt about that, but not necessarily at ease. He can be awkward with his grandkids, shaking hands with kids who are a little young for it. He's always saying to me and Eleanor and Katharine things like "Never been any damn good with babies." Which is weird when you are one of his babies.

Nick understands that my biggest fear is that I will become my dad. That I'll be a broke writer-mom with some hideous growth sprouting up from my shoulder, a second head but with no eyes or features, just a head that I brush off in conversation when people bring it up or suggest perhaps seeing a doctor, eager to get back to talking about my latest profile for *The New Yorker.* I think about Crazy Kate and Dagwood, and then my dad and then me, three generations of us, and I look at Hudson eating his chocolate in a cup and think how much Hudson seems like a writer's name.

I recently reread the piece of my father's from *Harper's* magazine called "Prufrock with a Baedecker," about St. Louis. In it he claims that St. Louisans are forever trying to recapture a past that he believes was never what they thought it was. "Old cities, like old families, obviously shabby, presumptively genteel, sustain themselves on dreams of vanished grandeur and it may be better to leave such dreams intact." It's a really good piece. The guy can write. I ask him, Do you believe dreams should be left intact? Of course I'm talking about my mother. Of course I'm talking about the fantasies, the dreams, the myths, the delusions, the denial around my mother's alcoholism. Maybe asking, Has it all been worth it? He says he doesn't anymore, that he never did, that he and Lewis Lapham, the editor of *Harper's* at the time, agreed that portraying a city in three or four thousand words was impossible and it was just one way to end the piece. "No," he says, "the truth should be told. The truth is not just for the young, and particularly in writing, the truth is everything.

"My God, people think fiction is a bunch of made-up flourishes, fanciful play. Fiction can do more than nonfiction, because it is the truth along with the artfulness and craft. If it's not the truth, it simply doesn't work, it won't fly, and the reader will know in an instant, well, this writer simply doesn't know the layout of this town or how a summer night might feel in a certain part of Montana, whatever it is. Fiction allows you to get as close as you want to actual facts, happenings, and then move away from it. There's artfulness and craft in nonfiction, no question, but you can't do what I just mentioned, which is big."

I can't help feeling that what Dad likes about fiction is the power of it, the power of being, essentially, more beautiful, more charming, smarter, better than, the truth.

"Almost . . . superior?"

He laughs. "Well said, Jean-Joe."

We talk of two-leveling: writing a story using another story as the base or first level of your story, like Joyce using the *Odyssey* as a first level for *Ulysses*. He hops back to the subject of Zelda and tells me about some new stuff he's gotten for his book from an old *Esquire* piece titled "A Summer with F. Scott Fitzgerald."

"You don't wreck a life to create a novel," he blurts. "You don't ruin a woman like Zelda who was a genius in three different directions." I hear it again. It's not that he thought he should have gotten to my mother's apartment sooner and saved her life. It's that he feels he killed her slowly, over the twenty-three years that they were married and then not married, because of the work he wanted to make, the two novels and everything else, and I think maybe he's doing an upside-down two-leveling: using the story of Scott's work taking precedence over Zelda's mental and physical health to come to terms with or write the story of his own artistic ambition and the unsightly fall of my mother.

"I GOT ONE WORD for you . . . 'Fitzgerald.'" When Nick says it one day I don't feel all that mad. At the very least it feels premature. He feels this is the cruelest, most powerful thing he can say, tapping into my greatest fear, of being as obsessive and unproductive and impractical as my dad. But articulating someone's biggest worry does not make it true. I am capable of making money, at least enough to survive. I take care of our son and I produce actual writing. Mommy just bought herself two teeth, muthafucka! Scrappiness has seen me through years when I wasn't getting paid. He is right in thinking, What kind of maniac would endure all that just for a shot at the bigtime? Or in my case, what kind of jerk would spend months writing a play just to put it on in my living room for one night and have a fantastic time doing it? The very thing that has gotten me here is the thing he despises, the thing he'd rather avoid if he can by not seeing my dad, the thing he lacked to keep going with painting: insanity.

I say my parents lived in the past, but to tell this story, I was, as my husband loved to point out, living in the past. Spending, in other words, every day of *my* life in the past, my past, my parents' past, even my grandparents' past, the past of my hometown, St. Louis, Jesus it never ends, the past! It just keeps going and going and going. I admit it; I'm lured in by stories, telling them, capturing events and people and molding them, making people laugh. And I am like both of them.

THE MARRIAGE ENDED. Maybe because we never should have gotten married. We were nothing alike. The way I look at it, though, is that I might never have become a mother if we hadn't been together. If I don't make any mistakes, I don't live, essentially. I miss out. The things that are wrong with me, the things I struggle with, are the things that define me. I have not changed in the way that I relate to struggle more than I do ease. This is, I suppose, my beef with sunshine. With Los Angeles. Was he right to quiver when he heard that there was a time when I owned one knife, a single spoon and two plates—at age thirty? Did he think that I would prefer to spend the day writing when I had a babysitter, over going out to lunch and a movie with him? Did he feel I loved to poke around on my computer, jotting down ideas and working on plays, more than I loved him? Maybe he did. Did he feel the only person for whom I would happily sacrifice a day of working was my son? I don't know. I do know that I now get to try to figure out how to be a writer and a parent. I get to try to figure out how to put my child before writing.

I have to let my father read this book and it is terrifying to think that I will hurt him with it. Am I doing exactly what he claims Fitzgerald did to Zelda and what I suggest he did with Mom, sacrificing him for my writing? Am I saying he put writing before all of us? All my father has done has been to show me wild enthusiasm and encouragement as a writer. I would never want to hurt him. I admire his writing and know I am not half the thinker or writer he is. His support of my writing was never about the writing for me. It was the love from my dad. And therefore, I have to agree with Eleanor and Katharine and Julia that I don't care all that much about his writing. I want him to be my dad.

———

WRITING IS A CHOICE. Does this make it all worse, the knowledge that you have other options, or does this make it better? A lot of days I've gotten to eat lunch at home and this is a really big perk in my opinion. When you're good and ready to take a break, you stroll into your kitchen and open the refrigerator door and poke around leisurely. "What am I in the mood for?" This is not a feeling people in offices get to have much. What's fast? What's cheap? What's on the way to the pharmacy where I'm picking up my antidepressants? This is how most people have lunch. To have lunch at home is a huge luxury. To cook a little something, prepare a sandwich in your own time, with just the right amount of tomatoes and a little of that basil one of your friends brought over the night before. And then grill it. To enjoy a little chocolate ice cream in a bowl in front of the newspaper before you go back to work. This is a nice way to live. To hang around bowls of chocolate ice cream and ideas all day can be worth it. It is a way that some people will never understand. So it seems writing is what Zelda said it was in the therapy session:

"Something may be a sort of fulfillment of yourself, and it may not be great to other people, but it is just as essential to yourself as if it is a great masterpiece."

My days so far as a small-time writer have been just that, essential to me as if they are a great masterpiece.

Did I just quote Zelda Fitzgerald?

ACKNOWLEDGMENTS

Thank you to the following people, who fall into three categories: terrific readers, terrific friends/family, people who have ignored the loud voice of reason and taken a gamble on me: Hollywood Hudson, Caroline and Jim Hays, Henry Tenney and his terribly petite publicists, Louisa and Baird Tenney, David McCormick, Ira Glass, Julie Snyder, Sarah Koenig, Geoff Kloske, Bell Chevigny, Alexander Chee, Rosanna Bruno, Sophia Ramos, Giana Catherine Allen, Linda Labella, Tracy Martin, Phantom Theater, Lois Tryk and Kurt Bier, Tammi Cubilette, Jenna Hornstock, Leah Allen and Mike O'Neil, David Rosenthal, Orlagh Cassidy and Nico Sidoti, Anne Magruder, Sara Goodman and Mott Hupfel, all the people who've ever lent me money or let me write in their house, the town of Warren, Vermont, especially Jane and Peter Schneider, Steve Badanes and Dave Sellers, and the New York Foundation for the Arts.